1001 Stranger Things Facts

Blake Dylan

Introduction

The ultimate trivia book for all Stranger Things superfans. 1001 Stranger Things Facts includes fascinating trivia on auditions, the many influences of Stranger Things, props, Easter eggs, music, special effects, cast & crew, mistakes, behind the scenes, the 1980s, cars, fashions, early plans for the show that never happened, fan theories, science, production design, locations, food, and an awful lot more. Unlock the curiosity door and prepare to explore 1001 Stranger Things Facts!

(1) Joe Keery was working as a waiter when he got the part of Steve Harrington. He had endured dozens of unsuccessful auditions before Stranger Things.

(2) The relationship between Mike Wheeler and Eleven in season one of Stranger Things is partly inspired by the friendship between Oskar and Eli in the 2008 film Let the Right One In. Let the Right One In is an acclaimed Swedish fantasy/horror film about a bullied eight year-old boy who strikes up a friendship with a girl who has a mysterious secret.

(3) In the first episode of season one, Hopper tells Joyce that a bird landed on Eleanor Gillespie's head (because it thought her hair was a nest). Eleanor and Alessa Gillespie are both the names of characters in the Silent Hill franchise.

(4) Billy Hargrove's look is largely inspired by the character of Randall Flagg in Stephen King's novel The Stand. Randall Flagg has long hair and likes denim.

(5) Stranger Things 3 had 2,500 special effects shots. This was 500 more than Stranger Things 2.

(6) Shannon Purser was working in a cinema when she got the part of Barb Holland.

(7) Lucas dons a cap of an Italian cycling team (Ceramiche Ariostea) in Stranger Things 3. This is a reference to the 1979 coming of age drama Breaking Away. Breaking Away, which features a cycling obsessed character who pretends to be Italian, is set in Indiana - just like Stranger Things.

(8) The Starcourt Mall in Stranger Things 3 is really Gwinnett Place Mall - an abandoned mall that the production team found in Atlanta. Netflix leased 20% of the empty and derelict Gwinnett Place Mall to renovate and create the authentic eighties mall we see onscreen in Stranger Things 3.

(9) Ross and Matt Duffer, who created Stranger Things and

write and direct many of the episodes, are brothers from North Carolina.

(10) The music when Hopper and Joyce arrive at the fair in Stranger Things 3 evokes the start of the eighties cartoon Dungeons & Dragons. This cartoon's intro began with the characters arriving at a fair.

(11) Finn Wolfhard as Mike Wheeler has the most lines of dialogue out of the cast in season one. He has 433 lines in the first season.

(12) When they began shooting Stranger Things 2, the crew noticed drones in the sky above the set attempting to capture footage. This was a far cry from season one - which was filmed in relative obscurity.

(13) Dustin and the boys play the arcade machine Dragon's Lair in Stranger Things 2. You do not see actual gameplay though (in so far as Dragon's Lair has gameplay - it was more of an animated choose your fate adventure) but rather the promotional reel the game used when it was launched.

(14) There was some doubt about Finn Wolfhard's participation in Stranger Things because he was cast in the film adaptation of Stephen King's IT around the same time. In the end he was able to do both. Wolfhard's casting in IT was uncanny because the Duffer Brothers had always dreamed of adapting this story themselves.

(15) After the kiss between Mike and Eleven was shot at the Snowball Dance for the finale of Stranger Things 2, the teenage and child extras gave Finn Wolfhard and Millie Bobby Brown a spontaneous round of applause.

(16) After production on Stranger Things 3 ended, Netflix eventually dismantled the Starcourt Mall set and took everything away. Locals in Atlanta felt this was a great pity as they'd rather hoped Starcourt could stay in place as a new

Stranger Things tourist attraction.

(17) Stranger Things was originally going to be called Montauk. Montauk is a village on the Long Island peninsula where a number of conspiracy theories have been linked to a decommissioned air force base named Camp Hero. The Duffer Brothers decided not to set in the show in Montauk in the end because they anticipated shooting by the coast and on the beach might pose some logistical (and weather) headaches. Most of the cast signed up when the show was still called Montauk. The Duffer Brothers said that David Harbour initially hated Stranger Things as the new title and much preferred Montauk.

(18) Downloads and streams of The Neverending Story song by Giorgio Moroder and Limahl increased by 800% after it featured in the finale of Stranger Things 3.

(19) Around 300 girls read for the part of Eleven before Millie Bobby Brown was cast in the role.

(20) Not a single real rat was used in the production of Stranger Things 3. All the rats are computer generated.

(21) The day that Stranger Things 3 first became available to stream, Maya Hawke turned off her social media in case people didn't like her character Robin.

(22) A part of Sleepy Hollow Farm in Powder Spring, Georgia, was used for the exterior shots of Hopper's woodland cabin (which was introduced in season two). This farm is a real place and has attracted some Stranger Things tourists.

(23) The first season of Stranger Things had a budget of $6 million per episode.

(24) David Harbour chipped a tooth shooting the sequences in Stranger Things 2 where Hopper is trapped in the vine encrusted Upside Down tunnels.

(25) Despite the important role Dungeons & Dragons plays in season one of Stranger Things, the Duffer Brothers said they never played this legendary roll the dice game themselves.

(26) The costume department on Stranger Things say they have to be careful not to dress Eleven in anything too fashionable because otherwise she ends up looking more like Millie Bobby Brown rather than the character of Eleven.

(27) In the original plan for Montauk (as the show was called then), the school science teacher Mr Clarke is a much more prominent and dashing character and based on Indiana Jones.

(28) Billy Hargrove has a Camaro. This is the car the baddie Buddy Repperton drives in Christine (a Stephen King book made into a film by John Carpenter).

(29) A lot of stuff naturally changed when the Duffer Brothers decided to drop Montauk as a title and location and set the show in Indiana. In the original plan for the show, Jim Hopper was going to live in a shack on the beach and the Byers house was going to be close to Camp Hero.

(30) The injured deer that Jonathan and Nancy find in the woods in season one was in reality an animatronic puppet.

(31) It was very warm and humid in Georgia when they shot the Halloween scenes for Stranger Things 2. Although the scenes were supposed to depict autumn and early winter, the cast were very hot.

(32) When shooting the emotional and tense classroom Demogorgon showdown in the last episode of season one, the kids all had the giggles and kept laughing.

(33) Steve Harrington was a lot meaner in the original plan for Stranger Things. Billy Hargrove, who was introduced in season two, is more like how Steve was conceived in the early plans

for season one.

(34) It was the suggestion of Millie Bobby Brown that Mike and Eleven should kiss at the Snowball dance in Stranger Things 2.

(35) Dacre Montgomery suffered from sunburn shooting the Billy Hargrove lifeguard scenes in Stranger Things 3.

(36) The map locations mentioned by Bob Newby in Stranger Things 2 like Jordan Lake and the Eno River are real places in North Carolina where the Duffer Brothers grew up.

(37) The Upside Down was called the Nether in the original scripts.

(38) It took about six weeks for the production team to renovate Gwinnett Place Mall and turned it into Starcourt.

(39) Steve Harrington was not originally going to be such a major character in Stranger Things. The original plan was to kill him off near the end of season one. The Duffer Brothers were enjoying the performance of Joe Keery though so they decided to keep him in the show and soften his character.

(40) When Dustin finally locates the missing Dart in the school in Stranger Things 2, the word 'EVIL' is written on the wall.

(41) Shooting the finale scene in Stranger Things 2 when Hopper and Eleven use the 'shark cage' to close the Gate to the Upside Down was a rough experience for David Harbour and Millie Bobby Brown. The swaying motion of the cage made Millie seasick and David Harbour said the guns he had to fire were absolutely deafening.

(42) The DemoDog that Dustin put in the fridge at the end of Stranger Things 2 is never mentioned in Stranger Things 3.

(43) The sequences with Eleven and the sensory deprivation water chamber in season one are influenced by Anna Torv's character in a scientific sensory deprivation water tank in the Fox TV show Fringe.

(44) Millie Bobby Brown said she had never encountered a record player before she went on the set of Stranger Things for the first time.

(45) The Palace Arcade in Stranger Things 2 is a derelict laundromat located in Douglasville, Georgia. The production team cleaned the place up and renovated the old store to look like an eighties arcade. It was so convincing that locals presumed it was a real retro arcade that was due to open.

(46) An early rejected plan for the Demogorgon was that its victims would bleed from the eyes and nose when it got close to them.

(47) The Byers fridge in season three has a drawing of Bob Newby as a superhero.

(48) In some of the early rejected designs for the Demogorgon, the creature was more plant like and had branches for arms with moss and vines.

(49) Look fast and you'll see that Mr Clarke has Beetlejuice's tombstone on his town model in Stranger Things 3.

(50) In the original plan for Montauk (as it was), Eleven was going to have a completely shaved head like Persis Khambatta as Lieutenant Ilia in Star Trek: The Motion Picture. However, in the end Eleven has more of a military buzzcut than a shaved head.

(51) The petal 'fangs' on the Demogorgon's face were designed so that they moved in a different way on each take.

(52) In the season one scene where the dead body of Barb is

found in the Upside Down, this was originally going to be a more gruesome moment. Concept art had Barb's ribs exposed and more gore and blood. It was decided thought to soften this moment somewhat. They also wanted Barb to be fairly intact and visible so that the audience would know it was her.

(53) The 2018 Starcourt Mall infomercial teaser for Stranger Things 3 includes a brief shot of the Tom Clancy novel The Hunt for Red October. This novel (later a film) is about a Soviet submarine commander who plans to defect. The inclusion of this novel in the teaser was a very big clue that the Soviets were going to be a part of the plot of Stranger Things 3.

(54) The real location for Steve Harrington's house in season one is 8253 Carlton Rd, Riverdale, GA.

(55) The special effects on season one were only completed days before Stranger Things was due to begin streaming on Netflix.

(56) The funfair hall of mirrors sequence with Hopper in Stranger Things 3 took fifteen hours to shoot.

(57) The white vest that Murray wears in the Stranger Things 3 finale is a joke reference to John McClane in Die Hard.

(58) In the episode E Pluribus Unum, Sadie Sink's sister Jacey was used as the younger version of Max in the flashbacks.

(59) In the car chase scene with Kali and her gang that opens Stranger Things 2, computer generated special effects had to be used to create part of the tunnel that collapses because the production team couldn't find a long enough tunnel in Atlanta.

(60) Mark Steger spent two months training and experimenting with the Demogorgon suit in preparation for the first season of Stranger Things.

(61) The fairground sequences in Stranger Things 3 were shot

in early autumn. The cast found it a chilly experience as they were wearing summer costumes.

(62) Shannon Purser did not know that Barb was going to be killed off when she signed to play the character.

(63) The first season of Stranger Things required around 150 wigs for the cast and extras.

(64) Millie Bobby Brown said she lost her voice five times during the Stranger Things 3 shoot.

(65) For his audition to play Steve Harrington, Joe Keery had to do the scene where Steve smashes Jonathan's camera.

(66) The Snowball scenes at the end of Stranger Things 2 took two days to shoot.

(67) It took a week to shoot the scenes in The Sauna Test where the kids trap Billy in the sauna.

(68) The moment in The Flayed where Joyce throws the gun to Hopper but it lands nearer to Grigori was not in the script. This was a goof by Winona Ryder but they kept it in because it was funny.

(69) In the scene in Stranger Things 3 where Steve finally wins a fight in the Soviet underground base, Joe Keery did the fight scene himself and did not use a stunt double.

(70) The production team on season one had to build an extra replica of the hall in the Byers' house so they could set fire to it.

(71) The music we hear when Eleven opens the music box in the Wheeler house in season one is Brahms' Lullaby.

(72) The Byers' porch swing is a reference to Sam Raimi's The Evil Dead.

(73) Over 350,000 people binged all nine episodes of Stranger Things 2 on the first day of its release.

(74) Mike tries to call Eleven at 7:40 p.m in Stranger Things 2. 7 + 4 = 11.

(75) The salt needed to float Millie Bobby Brown in the kiddie paddling pool scene in season one equated to 24 bags of salt.

(76) The Duffer Brothers killed Benny and Barb early in Stranger Things because they wanted the audience to feel as if none of the characters were secure.

(77) There is a Buzz Lightyear doll in Dustin's room in Stranger Things 2. Toy Story was still over ten years away from release though in 1984.

(78) Millie Bobby Brown only found out she would have to shave her head to play Eleven after the last audition.

(79) In the original pitch document for Stranger Things (still named Montauk at the time), Terry Ives is a bald paranoid male conspiracy theorist. The original (and discarded) plan for Terry Ives was used as the basis for Murray Bauman in Stranger Things 2.

(80) Natalia Dyer had a tough time shooting the brutal hospital battle that Nancy and Jonathan find themselves embroiled in during Stranger Things 3. The strobe of the hospital lights made her feel sick.

(81) Matthew Modine turned down the part of Dr Brenner when it was first offered to him because he felt the character was too vague. The Duffer Brothers made a personal (video) appeal to Modine while he was shooting a film in England and were persuasive enough to make him change his mind.

(82) The camera that Jonathan Byers uses in season one is a

Pentax MX. This camera was on the expensive side for Jonathan to own but chosen because it stressed how important photography was to the character. The Pentax camera belonging to Jonathan Byers required several identical models to be found or constructed because of the scene where Steve smashes it.

(83) The house of Heather the lifeguard in Stranger Things 3 is deliberately similar to Heather Langenkamp's house in Wes Craven's A Nightmare on Elm Street.

(84) Loch Nora, where the kids go trick or treating in Stranger Things 2, is the name of a real place near where the Duffer Brothers grew up in North Carolina.

(85) The scenes in Stranger Things 2 where Joyce is frustrated by the inability of the doctors to deduce what is wrong with Will clearly owe something to the medical scenes in The Exorcist where Ellen Burstyn is frustrated by the inability of the doctors to treat her possessed daughter Regan.

(86) The original pitch for Montauk proposed that a second season would take place 'ten years later' in 1990 when the kids were grown up. This is an idea that was obviously lifted from Stephen King's IT.

(87) Eleven improves her vocabulary in Stranger Things 2 by watching television. This is a reference to Madison the mermaid doing the same thing in the 1984 fantasy film Splash.

(88) The test models of the Demogorgon took over a month to construct.

(89) Millie Bobby Brown's longest line in season one is only seven words long.

(90) Priah Ferguson had never watched Stranger Things before when she was cast as Erica Sinclair.

(91) Stranger Things 2 had a budget of $8 million per episode.

(92) Gaten Matarazzo said that he came up with the idea of having a video game arcade in Stranger Things 2.

(93) Brett Gelman had to take some Russian language lessons for his scenes as Murray in Stranger Things 3.

(94) When we see Will's body floating in the quarry in season one, what we are really looking at is a female member of the stunt crew wearing Noah Schnapp's costume. They originally tried to use a dummy for this scene but it didn't look realistic enough.

(95) The special effects team found it complicated to make Dustin's pet Demogorgon Dart seem endearing because Demogorgons have no eyes.

(96) Natalia Dyer has the second largest number of lines in season one after Finn Wolfhard. Nancy Wheeler 346 lines of dialogue in season one.

(97) Most of the Starcourt Mall scenes in Stranger Things 3 made use of Gwinnett Place Mall's huge atrium space. The mall was perfect for the needs of the production because it had plenty of room for cameras and even a large balcony.

(98) The radio tower scenes in Stranger Things 3 include some of Maurice Jarre's score from Peter Weir's 1985 film Witness.

(99) The comic books Max and Eleven are perusing in Stranger Things 3 are Wonder Woman #326, Wonder Woman #324, and Green Lantern #185.

(100) Stranger Things 3 took eight months to shoot.

(101) The Demogorgon not having any eyes was inspired by the creature in Ridley Scott's Alien.

(102) The Duffer Brothers never considered calling the show 'Hawkins' because they felt that having a show named after the town in which it takes place was an idea that had been done too many times before.

(103) 37% of Millie Bobby Brown's lines in Stranger Things 2 come from The Lost Sister alone.

(104) Joe Keery as Steve Harrington has 326 lines in Stranger Things 3. This gives him the second most amount of lines (after David Harbour) of anyone in the third season. This is quite a feat given that Steve began as a supporting villain in season one.

(105) The Halloween party sequence in Stranger Things 2 required over seventy wigs for the extras.

(106) Dart was depicted by a rubber toy on the set of Stranger Things 2. The digital effects for Dart were added in post-production.

(107) The real location of Lonnie Byers' house in season one is 930 Garibaldi Street Southwest, Atlanta.

(108) The Byers' family dog Chester was absent in Stranger Things 2. The dog that played Chester was apparently quite disobedient during production of season one so they obviously decided life would be simpler without a dog on the set.

(109) In Dungeons & Dragons, thessalmonsters are a group of related creatures designed to resemble the hydra. The Mind Flayer could be described as having hydra-like qualities.

(110) David Harbour said it took forever to get in and out of the Hazmat suits that he and Winona Ryder had to wear for the season one finale (where Hopper and Joyce venture into the Upside Down to search for Will). As a consequence of this, the two actors tried not to drink any coffee or water so that toilet breaks would be minimal.

(111) Steve and Dustin leave a trail of meat in the woods to lure Dart in Stranger Things 2. Watermelon was used to depict the meat in these scenes because of its vibrant red colour.

(112) The scene where Barb coughs up a mouthful of goo in the Upside Down swimming pool in season one needed fourteen takes.

(113) Eggo sales went up by 14% after Stranger Things 2 came out.

(114) Max is supposed to be from California so some fake tan has to be applied to the pale skinned Sadie Sink.

(115) In the story pitch for Montauk, Mike Wheeler ventures into the Upside Down (or Nether as it was then called) to search for Will Byers. This was dropped though from the final scripts. We do not see Mike Wheeler travel into the Upside Down in season one of Stranger Things.

(116) Finn Wolfhard and Millie Bobby Brown both ate tic tacs before the kissing scene between Mike and Eleven in the first season finale.

(117) Joe Keery said he was very surprised when he got the Stranger Things 3 scripts and saw that Steve Harrington was going to be wearing a sailor suit for almost the entire season. He said he felt rather silly in this costume at first.

(118) Caleb McLaughlin, who plays Lucas Sinclair, very nearly missed the Stranger Things auditions because he was depressed at recent rejections in casting calls and didn't want to go.

(119) Suzie is reading A Wizard Of Earthsea when we finally see her in the Stranger Things 3 finale. A Wizard of Earthsea is a 1968 fantasy novel written by American author Ursula K. Le Guin.

(120) Dustin's mother is played by a different actress in season one. Tabitha Kilgore appears briefly as Mrs Henderson during Will's funeral. Catherine Curtin would take over the role in season two.

(121) Noah Schnapp was the last of the boys to be cast in season one.

(122) Sean Astin said he lobbied the Duffer Brothers for Bob Newby to get a heroic death. "I remember hoping that if I got killed off the show, it would be memorable."

(123) The Stranger Things titles and logo uses the ITC Benguiat font. This font was used on Stephen King paperback covers in the 1980s.

(124) The yellow Polly Flanders inspired dress that Eleven wears when the boys dress her up to go to the school and use the ham radio took a long time to find. It had to be a special dress because why would Nancy have saved it otherwise? There were several versions of the yellow dress made because it had to appear progressively dirty and worn the longer that Eleven wore it.

(125) Dustin names the hill for his radio tower Weathertop in Stranger Things 3. This is a reference to The Lord of the Rings.

(126) The kiss between Lucas and Max in the Stranger Things 2 finale had to be done a few times because they failed to capture Sadie Sink's reaction at first.

(127) Karen Wheeler is reading Tender is the Storm by Johanna Lindsey at the pool near the start of Stranger Things 3. The cover art depicts Billy Hargrove and Karen lookalikes as the lovers.

(128) Charlie Heaton had to wear hair extensions in season one because he burned some of his own hair on a candle while

in the bath.

(129) A poster for the classic Sam Raimi horror film The Evil Dead hangs on Jonathan's wall in season one.

(130) The sequence in the season one finale where Eleven takes out the soldiers in the school corridor feels inspired by a sequence in the animated film Akira where Tetsuo uses his powers to escape from heavily armed guards in a hospital.

(131) In the season one episode The Body, the doomed scientist who ventures into the Upside Down is named Shephard. This could be a reference to Alex Shepherd, a character in the video game Silent Hill.

(132) Steve's Scoops Ahoy sailor suit has a special holster for his ice cream scooper.

(133) Three Stranger Things cast members have been in the Alien movie franchise. Winona Ryder was in Alien: Resurrection, Paul Reiser was in Aliens, and Amy Seimetz (who plays Becky Ives in Stranger Things) was in Alien: Covenant.

(134) A copy Ernest Hemingway's The Old Man and the Sea can be seen when we first meet Hopper in Stranger Things. This book, about a cursed fisherman, suggests that Hopper is a man who has experienced plenty of bad luck.

(135) The boys had to do some scenes from Stand By Me and E.T. the Extra-Terrestrial in their Stranger Things auditions.

(136) Finn Wolfhard can faintly be seen to be warning (by saying "I'm coming in...") Millie Bobby Brown before Mike moves in to kiss Eleven at the Snowball dance in Stranger things 2.

(137) The radio at the cabin that Eleven and Hopper use to communicate in Stranger Things 2 is set on broadcast channel

11.

(138) The cannisters of green gloop that Steve and Dustin find in Stranger Things 3 are similar to the big canister of green liquid the students in John Carpenter's Prince of Darkness find.

(139) The opening of Stranger Things 3, where we see a team of Soviet scientists wiped out by their attempt to drill into the Upside down, is inspired by the end of Raiders of the Lost Ark where the Nazis try to open the Grail and meet a spectacular and grisly end.

(140) Aimee Mullins, who plays Terry Ives, competed in the 1996 Paralympics in Atlanta.

(141) The Duffer Brothers had a four and half hour conversation with Winona Ryder about Stranger Things/Montauk before eventually persuading her to take the part of Joyce Byers.

(142) The Duffer Brothers said that casting the right children in season one was the most important task they had. A gratingly bad performance from just one of the child actors could potentially have sunk the whole show.

(143) Erica takes a He-Man toy from Lucas' bedroom in Stranger Things 2. He-Man and the Masters of the Universe was a cartoon that ran on television from 1983 until 1985.

(144) You can hear a snatch of Boogie Man from the video game Fallout 3 in Stranger Things 3.

(145) Shooting on season one of Stranger Things began in November 2015.

(146) When Bob Newby asks (jokingly) if there is "treasure" at the end of Will's crayon map in Stranger Things 2, this is obviously a reference to the fact that Sean Astin was in The

Goonies.

(147) The scene in Stranger Things 3 where Mike tells Will Byers that it isn't his fault if Will doesn't like girls created some debate as to whether or not this confirmed that Will Byers was gay. Noah Schnapp judged the line to be ambiguous and felt the scene was about the fact that Will was less mature than his friends and wanted to turn back the clock to the time before he was trapped in the Upside Down.

(149) Millie Bobby Brown had no idea in her audition that Eleven was going to have super powers nor that she would be playing a major character in the show.

(150) Aaron Sims, who worked on the special effects and designs, said that the classroom duel between Eleven and the Demogorgon in the finale of season one was a complex sequence to capture. "The visual effects-heavy scenes were fairly difficult. In the last scene in the schoolroom, where the monster was brightly lit and it had to walk around and look threatening while being hit by rocks - that was all CG. The monster had to be thrown across the room and break apart. That scene was extremely hard for all of us. There was also the amount of time we had to do it - the disadvantage of TV is that the turnaround is so quick. That character was completely CG at that point, so it was very time-consuming. Breaking down the wall in the third episode was also the first time we did a scene that was fully CG. It was a challenge but exciting at the same time; we brought the character life in a unique way, and really showed how it was brought into this world."

(151) The pills we see Hopper taking in The Vanishing of Will Byers are Tuinal. This is an anti-anxiety medication.

(152) Gaten Matarazzo's voice changed so much during production on the first season that they couldn't use him for ADR. Automated Dialogue Replacement (ADR) is the process of re-recording dialogue by the original actor after the filming process to improve audio quality or reflect dialogue changes.

(153) Hopper reads Anne of Green Gables to Eleven in the cabin in Stranger Things 2. Anne of Green Gables is a classic 1908 children's book by L M Montgomery. The story concerns the adventures of Anne Shirley, an 11-year-old orphan girl.

(154) The scene in season one where Jonathan and Nancy find an injured deer in the woods and it is yanked away from something unseen was inspired by a near identical scene in the survival horror video game Until Dawn.

(155) Hopper's police deputies are named Powell and Callahan. Powell is a famous character in Die Hard and Callahan is a probable reference to Father Callahan from Stephen King's Salem's Lot.

(156) Finn Wolfhard was sick when the Duffer Brothers were casting Stranger Things and ended up auditioning via video from his bed.

(157) A lot of the younger cast members in Stranger Things have a stage background. Gaten Matarazzo, Caleb McLaughlin, Sadie Sink, and Gabriella Pizzolo (who plays Suzie in Stranger Things 3), had all appeared on Broadway prior to being cast in Stranger Things.

(158) Noah Schnapp as Will Byers has 115 more lines in season two than he did in season one.

(159) Eleven in the improvised sensory deprivation kiddie pool evokes the pre-cogs using a bathtub to tune in on future events in Steven Spielberg's film Minority Report.

(160) An early (jettisoned) plan for the Upside Down was that it could exist in a different time zone from our own reality.

(161) In the pilot script for Montauk, Barb Holland is killed on the beach rather than at a pool party.

(162) Finn Wolfhard shot IT: Chapter Two and Stranger Things 3 at the same time. He described this as exhausting but rewarding.

(163) The boys use TRC-214 walkie-talkies in Stranger Things. These had a radius of a mile and were popular at the time with construction crews.

(164) In season one, we see Mr Wheeler trying to adjust his television reception so he can watch the television show Knight Rider. Knight Rider ran from 1982 to 1986 and starred David Hasselhoff as a crime fighter equipped with a futuristic artificially intelligent car named KITT.

(165) Eleven is revealed to be a fan of Miami Vice in Stranger Things 3. Miami Vice was a police action drama show with Don Johnson that ran from 1984 to 1989.

(166) Sadie Sink said The Sauna Test was the most physically demanding episode of Stranger Things to shoot.

(167) Holly Wheeler is played by twins Anniston and Tinsley Price.

(168) In the scene where we see what happened to Terry Ives at the Hawkins laboratory to make her catatonic, music by Philip Glass from his 1986 album Songs from Liquid Days is used. The imagery of this sequence could be inspired by the cult film Koyaanisqatsi - which Glass scored in 1982.

(169) Millie Bobby Brown says she loves scenes in Stranger Things where she has to scream because Eleven is usually quiet with a fairly minimal amount of dialogue.

(170) Most of the studios the Duffer Brothers approached when they were pitching Stranger Things (or Montauk as it was at the time) didn't like the concept of a show that relied so heavily on children.

(171) Eleven's blonde wig in season one cost (believe it or not) $8,000.

(172) The initial plan to set the show by the coast in Montauk was inspired by Spielberg's Jaws. "We liked Montauk, because we liked the coastal setting," said Matt Duffer, "and Montauk was the basis for Amity, and Jaws is probably our favorite movie, so I thought that that would be really cool. Then it was really going to be impossible to shoot in or around Long Island in the wintertime. It was just going to be miserable and expensive."

(173) Barb Holland's glasses are a homage to Martha Plimpton in The Goonies.

(174) Hopper has to go Merril's farm to investigate the rotting pumpkin patches in Stranger Things 2. Merril is a character name in two Stephen King stories (Needful Things and The Body).

(175) The television set in the Wheeler house that Mike proudly shows Eleven in season one is a 22-inch Mitsubishi.

(176) In the first season of Stranger Things, the Duffer Brothers admit that entire scenes were shot and designed to evoke scenes in E.T. the Extra-Terrestrial.

(177) Dustin's 'totally tubular' catchphrase in season two is because Max is from California. The specific source is Frank Zappa's 1982 Valley Girl single.

(178) The Duffer Brothers have said that the Harry potter films were an influence on the Mind Flayer in Stranger Things 2. "Last year, we always referred to the Demogorgon as like a shark. Like Jaws — a shark in another dimension that would every once in awhile breach into our world and yank its victim back down into its dimension. [This season,] we wanted to talk about: Is there something higher up on the food chain? Is there something more sentient? Sort of the Sauron, the

Voldemort. So we started to talk about that. We started to talk about, obviously HP Lovecraft, and we started talking about cosmic horror. We talked about Clive Barker. We talked about what scared us, generally, growing up. And eventually, it developed into this Mind Flayer."

(179) There is a sly costume Easter egg near the end of Stranger Things 3 when Lucas and Max wear outfits worn by Eric and Donna in 'That 70s Show.

(180) The moment in Stranger things 2 where Steve wakes up in the car (which is being driven by Max) after his pounding at the hands of Billy and groggily says Nancy's name was improvised by Joe Keery.

(181) In the scene where Joyce has to paint an alphabet on the wall in season one, Winona Ryder did this in one take.

(182) The games in the Palace Arcade for Stranger Things 2 were all playable and real. The cast and crew were able to play on the machines between takes.

(183) In the first season of Stranger Things, Mike Wheeler is made to look a lot like Henry Thomas in the 1984 kids spy film Cloak & Dagger.

(184) When Joyce takes an axe to the wall in season one, this is a homage to Jack Nicholson in Kubrick's The Shining.

(185) The Demogorgon in season one was a mix of practical and computer generated effects. Mark Steger was inside the Demogorgon suit. "It was actually really loud in there," said Steger. "Even when the motors were turned off, there was this high-pitched whine. And there were 26 motors running the head, and when we were actually doing a shot, I couldn't hear directions. They would have to shout at the top of their lungs, and then maybe I would hear them. The suit probably weighed about 30 pounds or so, and you're completely sealed in. It's like wearing a wetsuit and covering your whole body."

(186) Millie Bobby Brown and Noah Schnapp pranked the costume designer on season one by pretending that she'd had a call saying her wedding venue was double booked.

(187) Gaten Matarazzo was the first of the kids to be cast in Stranger Things.

(188) The game of Dungeons & Dragons in The Vanishing of Will Byers foreshadows and anticipates the events that will occur in season one - especially in the case of poor Will Byers.

(189) The Duffer Brothers, despite their relative youth, considered themselves finished after the failure of their 2015 horror movie Hidden to attract any attention. The reviews were mostly decent but the film made just $310,000 at the box-office.

(190) When the DemoDogs sneak up on Steve at the junkyard in Stranger Things 2, this is a homage to Bob Peck's game warden being surprised by the Velociraptor in Jurassic Park.

(191) Brett Gelman as Murray Bauman has 66 more lines in season three than he did in season two.

(192) Over 900 boys were auditioned before they cast Mike, Dustin, Lucas, and Will.

(193) The Lost Sister's depiction of the Chicago skyline in The Lost Sister is too contemporary for 1984. The Trump International Hotel & Tower only opened in 2009 and the Blue Cross Blue Shield Tower was constructed in 1997.

(194) The Starcourt Mall set had an operational food court and real hot food was constantly prepared for background extras to eat in scenes.

(195) Sound designer Craig Henighan created the spooky sound effects for the Demogorgon in season one. "I think in

Alien they used cappuccino makers and peacocks amongst other sounds. So I try to be aware of those sounds and initially I thought I'd try not to make the Entity out of real animals or human sounds. I thought I could do it with dry ice and squeaks and other oddball sounds that I could record or that I've collected over the years. But, that sort of failed. A lot of those things just didn't sound right for this monster. I recorded my own voice and tried to manipulate that. I did a little bit early on with Dehumaniser and other plug-ins to get something working but that sounded a little too heavy-handed. I wanted it to sonically evoke creepiness and intellect. When we get into the flesh, I recorded splatty sounds of water hitting flour, and other splats. I also used some great stuff from Boom Library and my good friend Rob Nokes has done a lot of specific recordings for me over the years. I had other fleshy movement sounds and door squeaks, rubber yoga ball creaks. I did some dry ice recordings that are part of the Entity's bigger roars and screams."

(196) Parasyte, a horror manga series written and illustrated by Hitoshi Iwaaki from 1988 to 1995, was a probable influence on the Demogorgon. The first monster in Parasyte has a mouth that opens like flesh flower petals and is very similar to the Demogorgon.

(197) The Soviet scientist at the start of Stranger Things 3 is put in a choke-hold like the Imperial officer was put in a choke-hold by Darth Vader in Star Wars.

(198) The music during the home-made sensory deprivation tank scene in The Bathtub is Fields of Coral from the 1996 album Oceanic by Vangelis.

(199) Sadie Sink and Millie Bobby Brown asked the Duffer Brothers to make Max and Eleven best friends in Stranger Things 3 because they wanted more scenes together.

(200) Charlie Heaton said that he was rather disappointed to get hardly any scenes with Noah Schnapp in Stranger Things

3.

(201) Denis Villeneuve's 2013 movie Prisoners, a drama about a child that goes missing, was an influence on season one of Stranger Things. The Duffer Brothers liked the idea of taking a story like this and giving it a big sci-fi twist.

(202) Bellwood Quarry was used for the quarry scenes in Stranger Things. The Walking Dead, which is also shot in Atlanta, has also shot a number of scenes at Bellwood Quarry.

(203) Billy's Camaro car in Stranger Things 2 appears to have automatic windows in some scenes and crank windows at other times. This is obviously a consequence of using two different cars for shooting.

(204) David Harbour said he used to play Dungeons & Dragons when he was a kid.

(205) Matt Duffer explained Karen Wheeler not deducing that Eleven was in the basement of her house in season one the following way - "She's happily oblivious. She has no reason to think anything. My mindset is, when we were growing up, and we were making these really bad nerdy movies, we would just wander off. We were left alone all day. They didn't come into our world. We didn't want our parents coming into our world. Mike and his friends spend an obscene amount of time in his basement playing these never ending Dungeons and Dragons campaigns. Karen just doesn't come down there. She has no reason to be concerned."

(206) Cara Buono wore waterproof mascara so that Karen Wheeler's eye make-up wouldn't smear during the swimming pool scenes in Stranger Things 3

(207) Asteroids, Galaga, Centipede and Pac-Man are among the games that feature in the Palace Arcade.

(208) The music score in Stranger Things is composed by

Michael Stein and Kyle Dixon of Survive (S U R V I V E). Survive is an electronic synth group.

(209) The Duffer Brothers, when they first pitched the concept of Stranger Things, cut together a mock trailer of eighties movie clips with a John Carpenter score. "To test-drive the concept, we threw together a quick mock-trailer for the show, editing together clips from more than 25 classic films. We then scored this fake trailer with John Carpenter music, using some of our favorite songs from The Fog to Escape From New York. As soon as we heard John Carpenter's eerie synth drones play over shots from E.T., we got major goosebumps. It worked, big time."

(210) The Duffer Brothers also put a Survive song (named Dirge) over the mock trailer and found that it was a perfect match. Michael Stein and Kyle Dixon were therefore hired to compose the music for Stranger Things.

(211) "The first thing we saw was the trailer they made with our song in it before they shot anything," said Kyle Dixon. "We saw a little look-book with inspiration, synopsis, character stuff, we saw scripts before they had even done any casting. We were doing demos for themes prior to casting. They actually used some of the demos against the auditions to help decide, I guess, both on the music and who they would get to act in it. So we were involved from the very beginning, I would say. Not the very beginning but early on. They had only written maybe two or three episodes when we came on. They definitely wanted the music to be a big part of it and that's why they brought us in so early. So we worked on it for a fairly substantial amount of time because they wanted to make sure it was right which was good for us because we were just learning the ropes on scoring. It definitely helped us figure out what we were doing."

(212) The horror writer HP Lovecraft is an influence on Stranger Things. Lovecraft's work is full of creatures so indescribably hideous that one look at them would lead to

insanity.

(213) Millie Bobby Brown said it was very difficult to scream in the Sea Trek helmet for the sensory deprivation underwater sequence in season one.

(214) The Stranger Things creators and producers had to ask Dan Aykroyd for permission to use the Ghostbusters costumes in season two. Dan Aykroyd was happy to give consent and said he enjoyed Stranger Things. In a quirk of fate, Finn Wolfhard would later be cast in a new Ghostbusters film.

(215) Alexei wanting the cherry slushie in Stranger Things 3 is a reference to the film Heathers. In that film, Winona Ryder's character wanted a cherry slushie.

(216) In the French language version of Stranger Things, Lucas is dubbed in the first season by a female voice actor.

(217) Joe Keery was hurt by a breakaway prop plate being smashed over his during the fight scene between Steve and Billy near the end of Stranger Things 2.

(218) The Byers house in Stranger Things is a real house that the production team found in a rural part of Georgia. Only the exteriors are used though. The interiors are shot in the Screen Gems studio in Atlanta.

(219) Scoops Ahoy is a fictional company. It was based on Baskin-Robbins.

(220) Dustin calls himself 'Gold Leader' on the walkie-talkie in Stranger Things 3. Gold Leader is the callsign of Lando Calrissian in Return of the Jedi.

(221) The background extras in the Starcourt Mall scenes in season three include someone dressed like eighties singer Boy George.

(222) Dacre Montgomery had to have 33 prosthetic wounds applied to him as Billy Hargrove in Stranger Things 3.

(223) The Duffer Brothers stipulated that the Starcourt Mall had to have Scoops Ahoy, a Gap, and something like a Glamour Shots photo studio. The rest of the stores though they left in the hands of the production team.

(224) The Upside Down is patently influenced by the desolate planet LV-426 from Ridley Scott's Alien and James Cameron's Aliens.

(225) The Duffer Brothers think they should have used the Palace Arcade more in Stranger Things 2. They don't think they came up with enough arcade scenes.

(226) The shot of Will Byers looking into the bathroom mirror at the end of the season one finale, after he deduces that the Upside Down is not finished with him yet, is designed as a homage to the scene at the end of the original run of Twin Peaks when Agent Cooper looks into the mirror and we see that he has been infected with evil.

(227) Patrick Henry Academy at 109 S. Lee St. in Stockbridge was the location for Hawkins High/Middle School. This was a real school but one that closed because of a mould problem in the building.

(228) During the production of Stranger Things 3, Dacre Montgomery got his hand stuck to a table during lunch because of all the glue that had been applied to his fake prosthetic wounds.

(229) It took three days to film the last fight between Hopper and Grigori in the finale of Stranger Things 3.

(230) One of the articles in the news clip at the end of Stranger Things 3 quotes a man named Dean Zimmerman. Dean Zimmerman is the Stranger Things editor.

(231) Stranger Things casting director Carmen Cuba said of Millie Bobby Brown's audition - "An agent who knows my taste very well sent me info on her and I was intrigued so we had her tape. She's based in London so she taped herself and it was amazing — really emotional and intense, lots of tears — and that's where we started with the process. From there, we had her do additional material, gave her some direction over email, and eventually, Skyped with her then brought her to the US to test with our other kids. She did the entire Skype in an American accent and it was so good we didn't even notice until the very end. Millie was very impressive on all levels."

(232) The Sauna Test sequences in the sauna required three months of storyboarding and stunt choreography.

(233) Eleven usually bleeds from the left nostril.

(234) Dacre Montgomery wore his own Saint Christopher necklace while playing Billy Hargrove.

(235) Douglasville City Hall at 8485 Courthouse Square was used as the interior and exterior location for the Hawkins Police Station.

(236) The Duffer Brothers originally planned to kill Eleven for good in the first season finale.

(237) Billy calls a kid "lard ass" at the pool in Stranger Things 3. This is obviously a reference to the pie eating contest sequence in Stand By Me.

(238) The Georgia Mental Health Institute (later Emory University's Continuing Education Department) was used for the exteriors of the Hawkins Department of Energy. The Georgia Mental Health Institute opened in 1965 but was closed in 1997.

(239) Eleven was a much more violent character in the early

plans for (what eventually became) Stranger Things.

(240) The Duffer Brothers said they felt some guilt at killing Barb off so quickly because it was Shannon Purser's first acting job and she was so nice to work with.

(241) The Duffer Brothers said that, out of all the boys in season one, Mike Wheeler was the closest to what they were like at that age.

(242) The original pitch for Montauk (as it was then) was this - 'Described as a love letter to the '80s classics that captivated a generation, the series is set in 1980 Montauk, Long Island, where a young boy vanishes into thin air. As friends, family and local police search for answers, they are drawn into an extraordinary mystery involving top-secret government experiments, terrifying supernatural forces and one very strange little girl.'

(243) The doomed lifeguard in Stranger Things 3 is called Heather. In the Winona Ryder film Heathers, the first girl to die is named Heather.

(244) David Harbour said the season one Demogorgon was genuinely scary to encounter on the set.

(245) In the pilot script for Montauk, Jonathan Byers works in a cinema.

(246) Millie Bobby Brown had to wear a Sea Trek helmet and descend into a water tank for real to shoot the scene where Eleven enters the water tank in the lab for Dr Brenner. Her helmet was equipped with a radio through which the Duffers could talk to her.

(247) The scenes in Stranger Things 3 where Steve and Robin are delirious from the effects of the Soviet truth serum were complex to act and edit because the 'delirium' of the characters had to have continuity and be consistent.

(248) Eleven has some Reebok High Top White Sneakers in Stranger Things 3.

(249) The Silent Hill video game series was a very obvious influence on the Upside Down. The town of Silent Hill is a fog bound haunted place where (unseasonal) snow and dust seems to cloud everything in murk and mystery.

(250) Dustin packs some Debbie Nutty Bars for Operation Mirkwood in season one. These are wafers sandwiched together in a peanut butter mixture and covered with a chocolate-colored coating.

(251) Millie Bobby Brown estimated that she only had to eat the equivalent of a couple of Eggos shooting season one.

(252) Dart was voiced by the sound designer Craig Henighan.

(253) Caleb McLaughlin is the oldest of the 'kids' in the cast. He was born in October, 2001.

(254) In the pilot script for Montauk, Benny's Burgers was going to be a fish and chip diner. The fact they didn't do this must have been a relief to Millie Bobby Brown because the pilot script had a scene where a starving Eleven bites the head off a raw fish in Benny's diner.

(255) Gaten Matarazzo, Caleb McLaughlin and Sadie Sink all knew each other before Stranger Things because their paths had crossed on Broadway.

(256) Dacre Montgomery improvised the moment in Stranger Things 2 where Billy Hargrove takes a cookie while flirtatiously chatting with Karen Wheeler in the kitchen.

(257) Stranger Things 2 began production with a secret codename in an attempt to avoid media attention and potential spoilers.

(258) In season one, when Eleven takes the Eggos from the store, you can see a few cars go past outside that are way too modern for 1983.

(259) David Harbour said that Nick Nolte in old cop movies was an influence on Jim Hopper.

(260) Dustin wears a Science Museum of Minnesota dinosaur hoodie in Stranger Things 2. The Science Museum of Minnesota's website crashed after season two came out because the demand for these hoodies was so great.

(261) The Duffer Brothers had only written a couple of episodes when Kyle Dixon and Michael Stein were hired to do the music.

(262) The video game series Uncharted was an influence on Stranger Things.

(263) David Harbour said that the kids in the cast were amused by the wall telephones with super long cords when they went on the season one sets for the first time.

(264) The Duffer Brothers said that many of the Easter eggs in season one were unconscious.

(265) The decor in the Wheeler house has similar patterns to the decor of the house in the 1982 film Poltergeist.

(266) Dacre Montgomery took one of Billy's tank tops as a memento when shooting on Stranger Things 3 ended.

(267) The work of Polish painter Zdzislaw Beksinski was a very big influence on the look of the Upside Down.

(268) The Hawkins Community Pool scenes in season three were shot at South Bend Pool at 2000 Lakewood Ave. SE. This was a real operational pool situated conveniently close to the

studio.

(269) The Duffer Brothers said they never considered bringing Barb Holland back for Stranger Things 2. She did though influence the story in season two - specifically Jonathan and Nancy trying to get justice on the lab for Barb's parents.

(270) Ross Duffer said it was a great thrill him and his brother to cast Winona Ryder. "Winona came up very early on and was on one of our first casting lists that our casting director came up with, and we all fell instantly in love with that idea. Certainly there's nostalgia there, but this is someone we were huge fans of growing up, and it's someone we just wanted to see more of. And it's particularly someone we loved seeing in the supernatural genre. Not that she's not great in other things, like Girl Interrupted or Little Women. But Tim Burton was such a huge inspiration to us growing up and those movies were such a part of our rotation. It was also assigning us the idea of putting a movie star in this role because we always saw this as a big eight-hour summer movie. So to have someone like Winona, who has that movie-star presence where you just point a camera at her and she pops off the screen, it's not something most people have. So we were excited by the idea of her doing this."

(271) The exterior for the Wheeler house is Piney Wood Lane, East Point, Georgia 30344.

(272) David Harbour said he deliberately got heavy and out of shape for Stranger Things 3 because he wanted Hopper to feel even more slobby and disorganised.

(273) The monster clawing through the wall in season one is a reference to a similar scene in A Nightmare On Elm Street.

(274) Linnea Berthelsen (as Kali) has more lines in The Lost Sister than any other character in Stranger Things 2 has in any single one episode.

(275) The scenes where Eleven is in a black void of nothing in season one were very inexpensive and easy to design. "It's just an inch of water on the ground, said Ross Duffer, "and then we just hung up black curtains, and suddenly we're in Eleven's head. It's cool how you can achieve something that we think is such a big idea so simply."

(276) The shots of swimmers in the Hawkins pool at the start of Stranger Things 3 are a little riff on Jaws.

(277) Empire magazine said of Stranger Things 3 - 'Stranger Things 3 feels more like a big, mindless, summer blockbuster than the independent movie the first season was. But that's okay. After two hit seasons and a long absence, it's nice to see things turned up to Eleven, pun intended. There are shocking consequences here. Fists will be gleefully pumped in the air, jaws will drop out in awe, and tears will be shed for a number of reasons.'

(278) The 7-11 scene in Stranger Things 3 was shot near Tin Plate, down Milstead Ave in Conyers, Georgia.

(279) Project MKUltra is an important part of the story in season one of Stranger Things. It might sound like a fantastical conspiracy theory but Project MKUltra was actually real. 'The CIA is a goldmine for conspiracy theorists,' wrote Bigthink, 'and may hold the dubious honor of being the source of most of the conspiracy theories that end up being true. While some of the conspiracy theories that revolve around the CIA are wild speculation, a few of them are very real and well documented. Among them is a project with little scientific merit and significant ethical concerns called Project MKUltra. Project MKUltra was the code name for a series of investigations into mind-bending substances, techniques, and medical procedures. The goal was to develop truth serums, mind-control drugs, and determine what chemicals and methods had potential use for torture, disorientation, and espionage. The experiments started in 1953 and were slowly reduced in scope over the next 20 years before being halted in 1973. A

variety of experiments were undertaken to understand the effects of powerful drugs on unsuspecting subjects. These were often done in conjunction with hospitals and universities who claimed later they were not told what the goal of the experimentation was. At least 86 universities or institutions were involved in the acquisition of test subjects and administration of the experiments. Other experiments were also undertaken with sensory deprivation, hypnosis, psychological abuse, MDMA, salvia, psilocybin, and the mixing of barbiturates with amphetamines to sedate a subject before giving them a massive hit of speed in hopes of making them spill their secrets. Subjects included student volunteers, patients at mental hospitals, prisoners who both did and didn't volunteer, drug addicts who were paid in more drugs, and the occasional random person in addition to CIA agents who got unlucky. In 1973, then-CIA-director Richard Helms ordered all documents relating to MKUltra destroyed. However, 20,000 pages of documents were misfiled and survived the purge. In 1977, Congress organized the Church Committee and examined the records. As a result of the findings, Presidents Ford, Carter, and Reagan issued orders banning all future human experimentation without consent by government agencies, and some remittances were paid to those harmed by the tests. The project violated the Nuremberg codes, agreed to by the United States after the trials of Nazi war criminals, by administering drugs without informed consent. At least two people, Frank Olson and Harold Blauer, died as a result of being drugged without their knowledge. The true extent of psychological damage and death toll is impossible to know, as the records were mostly burned and the unscientific nature of many tests would make it impossible to determine what later events (for example, suicide) were attributable to the tests. So, there you have it. The CIA did use mind-altering drugs on unsuspecting civilian populations and those too weak to fight back and then tried to cover it up. While most conspiracy theories are far-fetched and debunkable with two minutes of thought, some of them are entirely true. MKUltra was a conspiracy between the government and many institutions to drug people without their knowledge and use anything learned from it for espionage purposes. Modern research into psychedelic drugs is increasingly benign, but we must remember that a great deal of what we know about them was discovered for the sake of making them weapons. A sobering reminder of what science can do without guidance.'

(280) The children in the cast in season one had to arrange their schooling around Stranger Things and were assigned tutors and a classroom on the set.

(281) Barbara Holland's first name is sometimes alleged to be a tribute to the heroine of Night of the Living Dead.

(282) The Duffer Brothers confessed they were somewhat in awe of Winona Ryder when they first started directing Stranger Things.

(283) Stranger Things was shot on a digital cinema camera but to achieve the vintage look a layer of scanned film grain was added to the colouring process.

(284) Stephen King's Carrie, a story about a girl with powerful telekinetic abilities, was one of but many influences on Stranger Things.

(285) Production designer Chris Trujillo was the man tasked with bringing the Upside Down dimension to life. "Dialing in a vision for the Upside Down (which we referred to as the Nether while conceptualizing it) was possibly the most creatively laborious and painstaking collaboration of the entire season. It was an object lesson in how tricky the alchemy of turning a shared fantasy into a physical set can be. It's funny because, from the beginning, everyone had a very clear sense of what the Upside Down should look and feel like and we could discuss it fairly clearly: like a dim, sick reflection of our world, murky darkness, a haze of spores floating in the gloom, vein-like vines overtaking all surfaces, like a disease is spreading over everything, etc, etc."

(286) Dacre Montgomery said he'd lost his voice by the end of Stranger Things 3.

(287) Millie Bobby Brown said she didn't like shooting the scenes where Eleven is alone in the cabin in Stranger Things 2. She didn't like being apart from the other actors.

(288) The Duffer Brothers were open to doing Montauk/Stranger Things as a movie but they always felt it would work better as a miniseries or television show.

(289) Dustin says "these aren't real Nilla Wafers" at the funeral of Will in season one. Nilla wafers are vanilla-flavored, wafer-style cookies. Nilla Wafers are often used in banana pudding.

(290) Steve Harrington using the term "KFC" at the Holland house in season two is probably an anachronism. Kentucky Fried Chicken had yet to rebrand themselves as KFC at the time.

(291) The io9 website wrote of Stranger Things 2 - 'If you liked season one, and pretty much everyone did, then you'll like this season just fine. Everything is turned up a bit, but the soul of Stranger Things remains what it was last season—a story about friendship, family, and giant piles of '80s nostalgia. Stranger Things had an almost impossible task when it came to following up on a first season that had near-universal acclaim. That it's still engaging, gorgeous looking, and smartly written is a truly impressive feat. The show didn't hit any reset buttons; it let every character grow and change, and it's just remarkable. This is a show growing naturally into itself and does everything to make the nine-hour commitment worth it.'

(292) Noah Schnapp is the youngest of the 'kids' in the cast. He was born in October, 2004.

(293) Matthew Modine thinks that Dr Brenner is not as bad as people make him out to be. "It's quite possible he is

passionately pursuing Eleven simply because he knows her potential and worries what might or what could happen if she were to get in the hands of someone that is truly sinister."

(294) The musician Father John Misty (Josh Tillman) was asked to audition for the part of Murray Bauman in Stranger Things 2. However, he wasn't interested and declined the invitation.

(295) The mouth of the Demogorgon was inspired by a snapping turtle.

(296) Pollywog is Old English for toad. Pollywog today means a tadpole in the larval stage of the life cycle.

(297) The Vanishing of Will Byers (set in 1983) has a Bluebird bus that was not introduced until 1990.

(298) EUE/Screen Gems Studios, where Stranger Things is made, is a 10-stage, 33-acre Atlanta studio complex.

(299) Hopper's trailer home in season one was in reality on some private property in Atlanta. It was - famously - purchased by the production team for one dollar.

(300) Psychokinesis or telekinesis is an alleged psychic ability allowing a person to influence a physical system without physical interaction.

(301) Stranger Things is scary but not TOO scary. The intention was to be like a PG-13 horror/fantasy film.

(302) Michael Stein and Kyle Dixon, the music composers, have a cameo in the video store near the end of Stranger Things 3.

(303) Maya Hawke was cast in Stranger Things 3 because she had the best chemistry with Joe Keery in the auditions.

(304) Craig Henighan said it was complex to come up with the sound effects for the Upside Down sequences in season one. "I knew The Upside Down would be dark and swampy but I hadn't seen any visuals. In my first conversations with Matt and Ross, I tried to find out what this alternate reality would be like. Is it supposed to be reverberant? Is it supposed to be dead dry? You try to establish ground rules about what it is you're trying to create. They said it would be wet, and give the impression of being wet, but they're not going to be walking around in the swamp. It had to be spooky and haunting but at the same time be familiar. I worked with these great forest recordings with trees creaking and I tried to use a bit of comb filtering. I didn't want it to sound like it was comb filtered though. I didn't want it to have this robotic sort of sound. Using GRM Tools, I went through and adjusted filter settings and found one that gave me a sound that was not really a delay or a slap but just added a bit of enticement. It's something between a reverb and a delay. So I loop recorded long passages of me plunking around on my sampler with these different sound files. Then I re-sampled those, and then re-sampled them again. By the second or third time, that's where the basis of The Upside Down sound happened."

(305) Eggo waffles were called Froffles when they first appeared in supermarkets.

(306) David Harbour had to wear a wig for Stranger Things 2 because his own hair was very short at the time.

(307) The scene in season one where Mike fakes illness so he can stay at home with Eleven is a reference to Ferris Bueller's Day Off.

(308) Stranger Things reminded some readers of Dan Simmons' 1991 novel Summer of Night. Summer of Night takes place in a small Illinois town in 1960 and revolves around a gang of boys who are around twelve years-old. The boys love riding their bikes and making dens in the woods. They gradually realise that some mysterious evil has awoken

in their town.

(309) The Duffer Brothers say there is much of their own personality in Barb Holland because they felt like outsiders at school themselves.

(310) There are posters for Q*bert and Crystal Castles in the Palace Arcade office in Stranger Things 2.

(311) The mall montage with Eleven and Max in Stranger Things 3 is inspired by a similar mall montage in the 1984 film Night of the Comet.

(312) Caleb McLaughlin had to do five auditions to get the part of Lucas Sinclair.

(313) Dustin wears his Ghostbusters sneakers to the Snowball dance in Stranger Things 2.

(314) The location for the Hawkins cinema is 2 N. Oak St. in Jackson. This is not a real cinema but a furniture store with its exterior altered to look like a cinema.

(315) The Demogorgon was built by Spectral Motion. This company worked on Guillermo del Toro's Hellboy films.

(316) Shawn Levy chose the Peter Gabriel cover of David Bowie's Heroes that we hear in the episode Holly Jolly.

(317) In season one and two, Hopper wears the hairband of his late daughter Sara on his wrist. From the finale of season two onwards, Eleven wears this hairband on her wrist.

(318) The articles you see on the Police Station bulletin board in the first season finale are titled The Boy Who Came Back To Life, Hawkins Lab Blocks Inquiry, More Heads Roll in Ongoing State Trooper Scandal, and Coroner Arrested for Falsifying Autopsy.

(319) The Weirdo On Maple Street is a reference to a Twilight Zone episode called The Monsters Are Due On Maple Street. The Weirdo On Maple Street could ALSO be a reference to The House on Maple Street. The House on Maple Street is a Stephen King short story in the compilation Nightmares & Dreamscapes.

(320) The hospital staff in Stranger Things 3 have the same uniforms and logos as the hospital staff in the 1981 horror sequel Halloween II.

(321) The Duffers said the stunt sequence with the (flying) van in The Bathtub was quite tricky to shoot and had to be done twice. "The van flip was a lot of fun... and very stressful. Like with the monster, we wanted to achieve the effect practically, without the use of CG. Our plan was to shoot the kids with a locked off camera as they biked across the street, and then merge that with a separate shot of a van flipping. Simple in theory — except for the part about flipping a van. We were initially told that there was no way we could flip a van of that size that high into the air. But we kept pushing, and our stubbornness eventually wore down our line producer, and he agreed to give it a try. The first parking lot test was a rousing success; explosives went off under a van, sending it rocketing high into the air. But... it was just a test. Now we had to replicate it on location with the cameras rolling. Easy, right? Not quite. One of the explosives didn't go off and the van skidded headfirst into one of our cameras, destroying both the camera and its lenses, and costing the production thousands of dollars. Our line producer was understandably loathe to try the stunt again, but we eventually wore him down again by promising that it would be heavily featured in the trailer (sorry, Iain — and also, thank you!). Thankfully, the second time was the charm. The van soared high into the air, our cameras captured it in all its glory."

(322) In one of the Stranger Things spin-off novels, it is stated that Dr Brenner had Eleven's real father drafted into the Vietnam War - where he was killed in the fighting.

(323) Gaten Matarazzo originally read for the part of Mike Wheeler.

(324) David Harbour said a 'Gandalf the White' style rebirth for Hopper at some point in Stranger Things was planned right from the start.

(325) The Demogorgon figurine owned by Mike Wheeler in season one was not produced until 1984.

(326) The vent crawling in Stranger Things 3 is evocative of Die Hard.

(327) Pyramid Head, an unfathomable beast in Silent Hill with no face, was an influence on the design of the Demogorgon in season one.

(328) Dustin has a certificate of Anti-Paranormal Proficiency on his wall from the Ghostbusters official fan club in Stranger Things 2.

(329) Mike Wheeler has a Teenage Mutant Ninja Turtle action figure in Stranger Things 2 that wasn't released until 1988.

(330) The car chase scene which begins Stranger Things 2 was shot in Atlanta but set in Pittsburgh.

(331) Noah Schnapp researched possessed people to prepare for Stranger Things 2.

(332) Charlie Heaton said he had forgotten all about his Stranger Things audition when the Duffer Brothers called him up at 4am to tell him he had the part.

(333) The budget for Stranger Things 2 was in the region of seventy million dollars.

(334) The character of Dustin Henderson was more generic in

the early script treatments for Stranger Things - he was more or less just supposed to be a geeky nerd. The Duffers were so taken with Gaten Matarazzo they allowed Matarazzo to craft Dustin more to his own personality.

(335) The Duffer Brothers said that Bob Newby was written as more of a 'dope' in their original scripts for season two and that Sean Astin fleshed the character out somewhat.

(336) Sadie Sink said that the Nikes in the Starcourt Mall sneaker stores were only on loan so were guarded very closely.

(337) Nancy has a Tom Cruise poster on her wall in season one.

(338) Hawkins and Hopper are both the names of characters in the 1987 sci-fi horror classic Predator.

(339) When Hopper sneaks into the morgue in season one, he encounters a state trooper reading Stephen King's Cujo.

(340) Gaten Matarazzo has cleidocranial dysplasia, a medical condition that means his teeth haven't come through. They wrote this condition into his character - Dustin Henderson.

(341) Mrs Driscoll has a Kit-Cat Klock on her wall in Stranger Things 3. Doc Brown has the same clock on his wall in Back to the Future.

(342) Paul Reiser accepted the part of Dr Owens in Stranger Things 2 before reading any scripts.

(343) The song playing when Hopper tries to revive Will in the season one finale is When it's Cold by Moby.

(344) Shannon Purser said she picked up some bruises shooting Barb's death scene in the swimming pool.

(345) Millie Bobby Brown's ability to cry convincingly was one

of the factors that helped her get the part of Eleven.

(346) Finn Wolfhard was ill when they shot the Snowball scenes for Stranger Things 2. He managed to get through them though.

(347) Roane County is fictional. There is no Roane County in Indiana.

(348) To generate a spooky atmosphere on the set, the crew played the soundtrack to Close Encounters of the Third Kind during shooting on the junkyard sequence in Stranger Things 2.

(349) The name of the video store company that Keith works for in Stranger Things 3 is Family Video. Family Video still exists to this day.

(350) The scene very near the start of The Vanishing of Will Byers with the boys playing Dungeons & Dragons in Mike's basement was the very first scene ever filmed for Stranger Things.

(351) The film that Steve sneaks the kids in to watch at the start of Stranger Things 3 is George A Romero's Day of the Dead - an enjoyably gruesome and cultish zombie film. The film was unrated so the kids would definitely not have been allowed in by conventional means.

(352) Some of John Harrison's music for George A Romero's Day of the Dead can be heard in Stranger Things 3 during the scenes between Steve and Robin.

(353) The sales of Eggos usually treble at Bradley's Big Buy grocery store (now part of the Piggly Wiggly franchise) in Palmetto, Ga, whenever a new season of Stranger Things comes out. This is where Eleven stole the waffles in season one.

(354) The translation of the secret Morse Code knock that Hopper and Eleven use at the cabin in Stranger Things is 'us'.

(355) The Duffer Brothers, well aware that The Goonies is one of Stranger Things' biggest influences, were reluctant to cast Sean Astin at first as they felt it would be too obvious.

(356) In real life, the Department of Energy is tasked with managing the United States' nuclear infrastructure and energy policy. The Department of Energy also funds scientific research.

(357) The first season of Stranger Things has a plot that is rather similar to a Twilight Zone episode called Little Girl Lost. Little Girl Lost is about a girl who becomes trapped in an alternate dimension thanks to a portal in her bedroom.

(358) The field used for the fair in Stranger Things 3 was reserved for a medieval recreation festival and completely empty when the Stranger Things production crew arrived.

(359) Hopper calling Alexei by the name Smirnoff in Stranger Things 3 is probably a reference to Yakov Smirnoff. Yakov Smirnoff was a Soviet born man who managed to flee the Soviet Union for the United States in the 1970s. He then launched a career as a comedian.

(360) In the scenes in Stranger Things where the characters are talking on walkie-talkies, the dialogue coming through the walkie-talkies is spoken to the actor on the set so they can react in a natural way.

(361) AV Club said in their review of season one of Stranger Things - 'What the Duffers lose in originality they make up for in the assured execution. The sibling team co-wrote and/or directed most of the episodes, and it's the rare example of a freshman television series that knows exactly what it wants to be from its earliest frames. The direction and cinematography are stunning throughout, and the series nails all the

appropriate period details from the costumes to the creepy production design. There's also the irresistible, Imaginary Forces-designed title sequence, which is rendered with vintage fonts and mottled with faux film grain. Balancing style and substance is always challenging for a series like Stranger Things, but the show is perfectly calibrated. It feels like watching a show produced during the era in which it's set, but with the craft of today's prestige television.'

(362) In the scene in Stranger Things 2 where Nancy is reduced to tears in the Holland bathroom, those are real childhood photographs of Shannon Purser.

(363) Hopper and Joyce's expedition to the Upside Down in the season one finale evokes the crew of the Nostromo exploring the bleak storm battered LV-426 in the original Alien film.

(364) Hopper's police jeep and uniform is based on Roy Scheider's Chief Brody in Jaws.

(365) Maya Hawke said she loved her Scoops Ahoy sailor suit and it was something she would wear in real life.

(366) Stranger Things 3 includes a blast of Neutron Dance by The Pointer Sisters. This song is from the soundtrack to the 1984 film Beverly Hills Cop.

(367) The Duffer Brothers said the alien queen in the 1986 film Aliens was an influence on the Mind Flayer in that they wanted the Upside Down to have a boss in the way that alien queen is the boss of the aliens.

(368) New Coke is featured in Stranger Things 3. 'New Coke first appeared in 1985,' wrote Yahoo, 'a reformulation of the popular soda that had been around for nearly a century in one form or another. The reformulation efforts came after Coca-Cola began losing a large share of the soft drink market, largely due to the competition from Pepsi-Cola and diet sodas.

In response, Coke began working on a new formula, and at first, the taste tests indicated positive results: tasters apparently preferred the new formula to both original Coke and Pepsi. The new soda was formally released on April 23, 1985, with a major press conference to announce the change. At first, sales went up as predicted, and some consumers did, in fact, like the new taste. However, backlash soon followed, starting in the South, who regarded Coke as a part of its regional identity and resented the change. Nostalgia for the "original" began spreading, and the controversy grew to an unexpected (and unexpectedly emotional) level. Ultimately, Coke decided to reverse its decision to reformulate. On July 11, 1985, the company announced that the original formula would return, much to the delight of consumers. The original formula was re-released as "Coca-Cola Classic" and sales skyrocketed. For a brief time in the early 1990s, Coke attempted to market "New Coke" again as "Coke II," but it was ultimately discontinued in 2002.'

(369) Coke brought New Coke back in 2019 for a short marketing release to coincide with Stranger Things 3.

(370) The Mind Flayer has some visual similarities to a monster called Amygdala from the video game Bloodborne.

(371) 64 million people streamed Stranger Things 3 within a month of its release.

(372) Georgia International Horse Park is where many of the woodland scenes in Stranger Things are shot.

(373) When we see Max and Eleven discover the body in the bath in Stranger Things 3, this seems a lot like a homage to a similar scene in the film adaptation of Stephen King's The Dead Zone.

(374) Joyce Byers has a Western Electric 554 Yellow Wall Phone in season one.

(375) David Harbour said that he would like to see Hopper and Steve have more scenes together.

(376) The gun of choice for the Hawkins Lab soldiers in season one is the Beretta 92FS.

(377) Dustin packs some Trail Mix for Operation Mirkwood in season one. Trail Mix is a mix of nuts and dried fruit to snack on.

(378) There is a copy of the 1984 Tom Hanks comedy Bachelor Party in Keith's video store at the end of Stranger Things 3. This is a sly joke as Paul Reiser was fired from Bachelor Party because the director didn't like his performance.

(379) The camouflage bandana worn by Lucas in season one was a suggestion by Caleb McLaughlin.

(380) In the news clip at the end of Stranger Things 3 we see a story by Brad Tobler. Brad Tobler is a VFX editor on Stranger Things.

(381) The car chase that opens Stranger Things 2 was inspired by car chases in the Christopher Nolan Batman films.

(382) There are some goofs in the arcade scenes in Stranger Things 2. The flat screen arcade machines we see are too modern and definitely not period accurate.

(383) In reality, Maxine Mayfield would not have had enough characters available to enter 'MADMAX' into Dig Dug's high score gallery. This is what you might call a very minor mistake (for artistic licence). You'd have to be an expert on eighties video game arcades to notice.

(384) Glennellen Anderson's Nicole is dressed as Ariel Moore from Footloose at the Halloween party in Stranger Things 2.

(385) The dimensional trouble in Stranger Things is similar to

the plot of the legendary video game Half-Life.

(386) The hospital scenes in Stranger Things 3 feature a goof when Mike gives Eleven some M&Ms and you can see some red ones. In 1985 there were no red M&Ms because of a (overblown) scare about red food dye.

(387) Old East Point Library at 2777 McGee Way in East Point serves as the Hawkins library interior. Butts County Probate Court at 25 3rd St. in Jackson was used for the Hawkins library exterior.

(388) There are some Sweet Valley High books in Eleven's bedroom in Stranger Things 3.

(389) The vials of green liquid the Soviets use for their Upside Down drill in Stranger Things 3 resemble the vials of plutonium Doc Brown uses for the DeLorean in Back to the Future.

(390) Stilts and puppeteers were used in season one to make the arms and legs of the Demogorgon unusually long and creepy.

(391) Robin's Scoops Ahoy uniform is like the Stay Puft Marshmallow Man in Ghostbusters.

(392) It was David Harbour's idea to give Hopper a hat. Harbour had a hat specially designed by Orlando Palacios at Worth & Worth. The hat was based on one that President Eisenhower liked to wear.

(393) Kyle Lambert produces the posters for Stranger Things. His brief was to replicate hand painted film artwork found in vintage movie posters from the 1980s.

(394) Millie Bobby Brown was shown a picture of Charlize Theron in Mad Max: Fury Road to see what her hair was going to be like as Eleven.

(395) The original plan for Stranger Things 3 was that Steve and Robin would end the season as a romantic couple. However, Joe Keery and Maya Hawke thought this would be too predictable. Maya Hawke suggested that Robin should be gay and everyone agreed that this was a more interesting plot.

(396) Noah Schnapp confessed that he didn't really know who Winona Ryder was before Stranger Things.

(397) Some cake frosting was used in Stranger Things 2 to give Will Byers a green tongue.

(398) Cara Buono said she lobbied her agent to get her the part of Karen Wheeler.

(399) There is a poster for The Muppet Movie on Suzie's bedroom wall in the Stranger Things 3 finale.

(400) David Harbour said he has always known how Stranger Things will end.

(401) The alley fight between Jonathan and Steve in season one is inspired by the alley fisticuffs between Roddy Piper and David Keith in the cult 1987 John Carpenter sci-fi film They Live.

(402) Eleven's dress and wig costume from season one is similar to Paula in the 1994 Super Nintendo classic Earthbound. Paula also has psychokinetic powers too.

(403) Female viewers make up 57% of the Stranger Things audience.

(404) Limahl had never heard of Stranger Things before they used his Neverending Story song in the season three finale.

(405) The Mind Flayer in season two was inspired by lightning and volcanoes - awe inspiring and unsettling reminders of how

powerful the natural world can be. "We knew from the Duffers that it would be humongous, like 50 stories tall," said special effects supervisor Christina Graf. "Since we had all these electrical disturbances last year in season one, where the Christmas lights were blinking or any sort of electrical light is blinking, we knew there were going to be storms in season two. The Shadow Monster is somehow connected to all of that energy, and then we determined it's gonna be like cloud-like or storm-like. We had conversations also with the production designer, Chris Trujillo, and we searched for a lot of references to storms and clouds and things like tornadoes."

(406) The Stranger Things title sequence is largely inspired by the titles for the 1984 film The Terminator.

(407) The spectacular and atmospheric sequence where Will Byers experiences a spooky Upside Down electrical storm outside the Palace Arcade was the first scene the Duffer Brothers conceived for Stranger Things 2.

(408) Peyton Wich, who played the school bully Troy in season one, said he got on so well with the other kids in the cast that it was rather difficult to get into character and be mean to them.

(409) The Sarlaac Pit in Return of the Jedi was the main inspiration for the design of the monster in Stranger Things 3.

(410) Dacre Montgomery improvised the moment in The Sauna Test where Billy head-butts the glass in the sauna. You can see the kids are genuinely surprised in their reactions.

(411) In the original story plan for Stranger Things (or Montauk as it was known as in the early days), Lucas was going to be a very troubled kid because his parents are going through a fractious divorce. This story thread was dropped though. We meet the parents of Lucas properly in Stranger Things 2 and they are clearly in a happy marriage.

(412) In the scene at the end of Stranger Things 3 where a

tearful Eleven reads Hopper's letter, Millie Bobby Brown only read the letter for the first time shooting the scene so her emotion would be more raw.

(413) Winona Ryder estimates that, as Joyce Byers, she spent about ten solid hours crying during the production of season one.

(414) Invasion of the Bodysnatchers was the biggest influence on Stranger Things 3.

(415) Sadie Sink and Millie Bobby Brown were allowed to choose the activities that Max and Eleven did in the season three mall montage.

(416) The sauna used in The Sauna Test wasn't hot in reality but it did contain some real steam.

(417) Elle (El) is the name of a character in Silent Hill: Homecoming.

(418) Director of photography Tim Ives said that Terminator 2 was an influence on the look of season three. "Referencing the look of T2 gave us a tone that's a little cooler at night, one where you see into the shadows instead of them being completely black. We wanted the details to be in the shadows and we wanted the contrast, but at the same time we didn't want it to feel flat or over-lit. This season is a rollercoaster ride. The kids are out of school and dressed in '80s fashion, which allowed for more colour saturation than previous seasons. Whilst Red gives us consistency across the seasons, we definitely wanted to keep it moody and mysterious at night. The Monstro sensor allowed me to do that whilst keeping a feeling of summertime abandon to the daytime exteriors. We still didn't want to look too modern though, which is why the lenses were important to add softer, rounder edges. We also altered the LUT to be a little less murky. The intent was still to make the show look pre-digital and as filmic as possible."

(419) The cast were allowed to fill up a 'goodie bag' from the Starcourt Mall stores at the end of shooting on season three. Sadie Sink however left her bag of goodies in her trailer and never got to take them home.

(420) Maxine Mayfield has a poster for the film Endless Summer in her room.

(421) The Duffer Brothers have said that the 2011 JJ Abrams film Super 8 was an influence on Stranger Things. Super 8 is set in the late 1970s and has a gang of children investigating a strange mystery in their small town.

(422) Nancy Wheeler is the name of a character in Judy Blume's young fiction novel Are You There God? It's Me, Margaret.

(423) The Duffer Brothers have a thirty page document which explains the general rules for the Upside Down.

(424) You can see some Trident gum in the store when Eleven steals the Eggos in season one. This gum was only released in 2001.

(425) Dustin's sneakers in the first season are K-Swiss Heaven S.

(426) When Brett Gelman as Murray Bauman drops some scrambled egg from his fork during breakfast with Nancy and Jonathan in Stranger Things 2, this was a real goof they decided to leave in the episode.

(427) Max and Eleven were going to have a food feast in the Stranger Things 3 mall montage but this never made it into the episode.

(428) The special effects team experimented with remote controlled rats before production on Stranger Things 3 but decided it wasn't practical.

(429) When Eleven levitates the Millennium Falcon toy in Mike's basement in season one you can tell it isn't a period accurate toy because it doesn't have the orange stickers on the back to represent the Falcon's engines.

(430) The Duffer Brothers said they had an awful time trying to think of a new name for the show after they dropped Montauk as the title.

(431) Mayor Kline has a '72 Mercedes-Benz SLC in Stranger Things 3.

(432) The mechanism which controlled the Demogorgon suit in season one was located in a backpack underneath the suit.

(433) The sequence in Stranger Things 2 where the Flayer possessed Will is tied down and questioned is inspired by gripping 'blood test' scene in John Carpenter's The Thing.

(434) Cary Elwes ended up very much the worse for wear when he went on one of the fairground rides in Stranger Things 3.

(435) Erica Sinclair is a My Little Pony fan. My Little Pony is a toy line and media franchise for girls developed by toy company Hasbro.

(436) The scene in Stranger things 3 where Hopper steals a Soviet uniform in the underground base is a homage to the scene in Raiders of the Lost Ark where Indiana Jones takes a German uniform in the Nazi U-boat base.

(437) You can see yellow road lines in Stranger Things but road lines in Indiana were white at the time the show takes place.

(438) Many stores you see at the Starcourt Mall like Sam Goody, Wicks N' Sticks, Waldenbooks, and Hot Sam Pretzels,

are now defunct and no longer exist.

(439) In the season one finale, Mike Wheeler was supposed to carry the exhausted Eleven into the classroom. However, Finn Wolfhard found it too difficult to carry Millie Bobby Brown so Gaten Matarazzo as Dustin did it instead.

(440) Before being cast as Bob Newby, Sean Astin auditioned to play Murray Bauman.

(441) Nancy coming to Dustin's rescue at the Snowball and giving him both someone to dance with and a comforting pep talk was based on a cousin of Ross Duffer doing the same to him at a dance when he was that age.

(442) Jonathan has a Timex Weekender watch in season one.

(443) The Duffer Brothers have said Elfin lied was an influence on Stranger Things. Elfen Lied is a Japanese manga series written and illustrated by Lynn Okamoto. It is about a telekinetic female who escapes from a lab.

(444) John Carpenter's The Thing was the biggest influence on the monster special effects in Stranger Things 3.

(445) Joe Keery said it was impossible to take toilet breaks during the shooting of the scenes where Steve and Robin are tied up back to back in the Soviet base. The ropes simply took too long to untie and tie again.

(446) Dig Dug is an arcade game developed and published by Namco in Japan in 1982, and later published outside Japan by Atari. The player controls Taizo Hori to eliminate the underground-dwelling monsters Pooka and Fygar by inflating them until they pop or by dropping rocks on them.

(447) When production on season one ended, Millie Bobby Brown took home some fake blood (for Eleven's nosebleeds) and Eleven's 011 tattoo.

(448) Erica crawling through the vents in Stranger Things 3 could be a reference to Bishop in James Cameron's Aliens crawling through piping conduits.

(449) The protesters outside of Mayor Kline's office in Stranger Things 3 have a sign that says - The pretzels aren't even that good!

(450) Bob Newby's death scene in Stranger Things 2 was originally going to be more gruesome but it was toned down somewhat in the end.

(451) Eleven's hair and clothes in Stranger Things 2 sometimes seem to be based on Alyssa Milano as Jenny Matrix in the 1985 Arnold Schwarzenegger film Commando.

(452) 13% of former Netflix subscribers rejoined the streaming platform specifically to watch Stranger Things 3.

(453) Over the course of the three completed seasons, Eleven is the character with the most screen time, just edging out Hopper.

(454) The Duffer Brothers decided to take Eleven's powers away at the end of Stranger Things 3 to add more tension. They were mindful of the fact that Eleven's powers had saved everyone in the previous two finales and didn't want the end of each season to be exactly the same.

(455) The main laboratory room close to the rift in Stranger Things 2 was based on NASA's Space Environment Simulation Lab.

(456) The costume designer on Stranger Things 3 said Robin's sexuality is hinted at by graffiti that Maya Hawke scribbled on her sneakers.

(457) When Nancy stops off at the store in Stranger Things 3

to find some bandages for Eleven's wound, the store is Bradley's Big Buy - the same place where Eleven stole the waffles in season one.

(458) Charlie Heaton as Jonathan Byers only has 138 lines in Stranger Things 3. This ranks Jonathan eleventh among the characters in season three with the most lines.

(459) Dr Brenner wore casual clothes in the early outlines for the character but Matthew Modine wanted Brenner to be more regimented and wear the same dark suit all the time.

(460) Gaten Matarazzo carrying Millie Bobby Brown into the classroom in the finale of season one was impressive because Matarazzo had an injured ankle at the time.

(461) The spores you see in the Upside Down sequences floating around are digital.

(462) Dr Owens quotes George Sarton in the episode Dig Dug when he says - "Men of science have made abundant mistakes of every kind." George Alfred Leon Sarton was a famous Belgian scientist.

(463) Cara Buono as Karen Wheeler has a fairly hefty 111 lines in season one. She would not get this many lines in seasons two and three though.

(464) The containers containing the green liquid in Stranger Things 3 open similar to the power cells on the Nostromo in Ridley Scott's Alien.

(465) The staff at the Hawkins Post witheringly refer to Nancy as Nancy Drew in a sarcastic way in Stranger Things 3. Nancy Drew is a fictional teenage sleuth who first appeared in literary form in 1930.

(466) Noah Schnapp and Caleb McLaughlin as Will Byers and Lucas Sinclair have (respectively) 64 and 74 less lines in

season three than in season two.

(467) Maxine Mayfield has the same brand of skateboard as Marty McFly in Back to the Future. The Madrid skateboard is their brand of choice.

(468) At the end of Stranger Things 3, we see that Will Byers seems to give his Dungeons & Dragons set to Erica.

(469) The newsclip at the end of Stranger Things 3 mentions controversies related to Dungeons & Dragons. In 1982, a young man named Irving Pulling shot himself and his family blamed his obsession with Dungeons & Dragons. An organisation called B.A.D.D. (Bothered About Dungeons & Dragons) and conservative Christian groups tried to get the game banned because they believed it celebrated demonology and witchcraft. The game was banned from a few school libraries in America but most people seemed to feel the campaign against Dungeons & Dragons was silly. The video game Doom and the Harry Potter films would later experience similar moral panics from Christian groups.

(470) When the toys belonging to Dustin come to life (in reality it is Eleven using her powers) in Stranger Things 3, this scene is similar to a scene in the 1985 Roland Emmerich fantasy film Making Contact.

(471) For the hospital scenes in stranger Things 3, where Bruce and Tom become Flayed monsters, the special effects team were inspired not only by John Carpenter's The Thing but also Frankenstein and the Hunchback of Notre Dame.

(472) There is a scene in season one where Mr Clarke is at home watching John Carpenter's The Thing with his date. Clyde E. Bryan worked as one of the Stranger Things camera assistants on this scene. Bryan was also a camera assistant on the actual movie for John Carpenter.

(473) Stranger Things is rated TV-14.

(474) Hanz Holzer's book Great American Ghost Stories is seen in season one. This is a goof because the book came out in 1990.

(475) Bob Newby has a JVC GR-C1 camcorder in Stranger Things 2. This is the camera that Doc Brown uses in Back to the Future.

(476) Stranger Things casting director Carmen Cuba said of Finn Wolfhard's audition - "Finn's first audition was from his bed because he was sick! The tape was also out of focus! But even so, he felt really dynamic and fun. And then we watched a few other audition tapes he did for other projects (one of them was for the Cary Fukunaga version of It) and saw he had great dexterity and range but also had a unique energy that made every performance specific to just him. He had an electricity that for me felt exactly like the real kids I knew at that same age who weren't actors. It was fun and slightly nutty with a commitment to the mission at hand. And that's what we thought would make the perfect ringleader. When we had them all in to chemistry read with each other it became even more clear because he basically ran the whole show on his own!"

(477) Eleven's nosebleeds are never CGI. A fake blood solution is simply put in Millie Bobby Brown's nostril.

(478) The blood from Billy's wounds in Stranger Things 3 was red at first but the Duffer Brothers then decided they wanted it to be black. This had to be done in post-production.

(479) A Red Monstro camera was used on Stranger Things 3 to give the season a bigger and more expansive feel. The lenses were designed though to add a certain softness and make Stranger Things 3 feel like something that was made before the digital age.

(480) Skin infections and animal bites were researched in

preparation for the make-up effects in Stranger Things 3.

(481) The Demogorgon is known as the 'Prince of Demons' in Dungeons & Dragons.

(482) When Hopper and Eleven clean up the cabin in season two, Hopper plays Jim Croce's 'You Don't Mess Around With Jim' on the record player.

(483) Dacre Montgomery caught the eye in his Stranger Things audition tape by dancing to Duran Duran's Hungry Like the Wolf.

(484) TIME magazine said of Stranger Things 3 that - 'The more permanent paradigm shifts of this season not only offer audiences a number of powerful dramatic moments, but it also sets the stage for an entirely new dynamic in whatever comes next while also concluding this journey in a fulfilling way that doesn't actually require another season. After having spent three years with these characters, these revelations feel fully earned, all while reminding both the audience and the characters that you can never go back to merely sitting in your basement playing D&D, no matter how much joy that would bring you.'

(485) Joyce Byers has a 1976 Ford Pinto - the same car the family in the film version of Stephen King's Cujo have.

(486) The Duffer Brothers and Millie Bobby Brown tried to be ambiguous about the fate of Eleven before Stranger Things 2 went into production so that her return would be more of a surprise. This didn't really work though and it was deduced very quickly that Eleven would be back.

(487) In the scene in the first episode of Stranger Things 3 in the car where a jealous Hopper is trying to get rid of Mike Wheeler, David Harbour had an attack of the giggles and kept flubbing his lines.

(488) The girls that Eleven gets revenge on at the mall in Stranger Things 3 by making an orange drink explode are the same girls that were mean to Dustin at the Snowball in Stranger Things 2 when he was looking for someone to dance with.

(489) Shawn Levy said it was surprisingly difficult to get permission to use a Michael Myers Halloween mask in Stranger Things 2.

(490) The Duffers often listen to film soundtracks when they write to get them in the right mood. The score for The Dark Knight was one of their favourites while they were writing Stranger Things 2.

(491) The video game The Legend of Zelda: Twilight Princess was an influence on the murky look of the Upside Down.

(492) Maya Hawke as Robin has a hefty 243 lines in season three. This gave Hawke more lines than Natalia Dyer, Charlie Heaton, Noah Schnapp, Caleb McLaughlin, and Sadie Sink all had respectively in Stranger Things 3.

(493) The Soviet doctor who interrogates Steve in the Soviet base in Stranger Things 3 is named Dr Zharkov. Dr Zarkov is a famous character in Flash Gordon.

(494) Natalia Dyer and Millie Bobby Brown both have the same stunt double.

(495) The Demogorgon was designed to have a very creepy silhouette.

(496) The Duffer Brothers were originally going to have Dustin and Suzie sing the Ent song from Lord Of The Rings in the Stranger Things 3 finale. It is believed this plan was scrapped because Amazon announced they were doing a Lord of the Rings TV series. Presumably, Netflix didn't want to be seen to be aiming a joke at another streaming platform.

(497) Hopper uses a Smith & Wesson Model 66 revolver in Stranger Things 3.

(498) The Mind Flayer monster attacking Starcourt Mall is a homage to the arrival of the T-Rex in the visitor center at the end of Jurassic Park.

(499) The character in Stranger Things 2 that became Kali (played by Linnea Berthelsen) was originally conceived to be a man.

(500) David Harbour was very surprised to get the part of Jim Hopper. He feared that Netflix might insist on a bigger name.

(501) Deadline suggested that Millie Bobby Brown was paid $350,000 an episode in season three. This (if true) would put her salary on a par with the adult leads David Harbour and Winona Ryder.

(502) The production team found the Georgia Mental Health Institute to be a very creepy and strange location. Production designer Chris Trujillo said - "Historically the building we shot as the exterior Lab was an experimental psychiatric facility, effectively a mid-century insane asylum, complete with these terrifying, long, low, stark white, underground corridors that linked the main building to what once were patients' quarters."

(503) Eleven uses the static of her television to try and contact Mike in Stranger Things 2. The television set was used as an inanimate source of foreboding and supernatural dread in the film Poltergeist.

(504) Matt Duffer named Cliff Martinez, Trent Reznor and Atticus Ross as influences on the music in Stranger Things.

(505) Mr Clarke's analogy about alternate dimensions is as follows - 'Consider an acrobat and a flea on a tight rope. The acrobat can move forward and backward along the rope. But

the flea can move forward and backward as well as side to side. If the flea keeps walking to one side, it goes around the rope and winds up where it started. So the acrobat has one dimension, and the flea has two dimensions, but one of these dimensions is a small closed loop. So the acrobat cannot detect any more than the one dimension of the rope, just as we can only see the world in three dimensions, even though it might well have many more. This is impossible to visualize, precisely because we can only visualize things in three dimensions. Creatures which are much smaller can travel to the extra dimension back and forth, while we cannot. In order to have access to tiny dimensions, you do need a lot of energy. The more energy you have, the smaller the entity that you can observe.'

(506) Charlie Heaton ended up with less lines in Stranger Things 2 than Paul Reiser and Sean Astin - which seems strange given that Jonathan Byers is supposed to be one of the original main characters.

(507) You can see a 1984 election sign for President Reagan outside the Wheeler house in Stranger Things 2. Dustin's mother is supporting Walter Mondale.

(508) The strange crayon sketches by Will Byers you see in Stranger Things 2 were done both by Noah Schnapp and the crew.

(509) The set decorators on season one trawled through dozens of thrift stores and garage sales to look for items that might be authentic to the middle America of 1983.

(510) Dacre Montgomery improvised the scene in Will the Wise where Billy grabs Max by the wrist. Montgomery and Sadie Sink worked on this moment together before the scene was shot so that it would be safe and Sink would be prepared.

(511) Four hundred extras were required for the fairground scenes in Stranger Things 3.

(512) So much salt was required for the kiddie paddling pool scene in The Bathtub that it gave Millie Bobby Brown a migraine by the time the scene was in the can.

(513) The casting of Paul Reiser as Dr Owens in Stranger Things 2 obviously trades on his part in Aliens, where Reiser played the corporate villain Carter Burke. Burke was ambiguous at first - just like Owens in Stranger Things.

(514) The Mind Flayer attacks Will through smoke in Stranger Things 2 like the Smoke Monster in Lost.

(515) Many believe the title theme in Stranger Things owes something to the airport abduction music in John Carpenter's Big Trouble in Little China.

(516) Millie Bobby Brown was recovering from a fractured kneecap at the start of shooting on Stranger Things 3. There were certain things she couldn't do. She couldn't, for example, ride a bike.

(517) When Jonathan trips over in Stranger Things 3 while getting dressed in the morning, this is a homage to Marty McFly doing the same thing in Back to the Future.

(518) Finn Wolfhard said he was ready to give up acting before he was cast in Stranger Things.

(519) Stranger Things 4 began shooting in February 2020 but production was then halted for several months because of the pandemic.

(520) The dummy of Will Byers season one that Hopper cuts into in the morgue was made by Justin Raleigh. Boston Children's Hospital use Raleigh's dummies to train surgeons.

(521) Dacre Montgomery researched bipolar disorder and split personalities in preparation for Stranger Things 3.

(522) A 2016 poll in Time Out named Hawkins as the fictional place where people would most like to go on vacation. King's Landing and Hogwarts were second and third.

(523) A record 26.4 million Netflix users watched Stranger Things 3 the weekend of its release.

(524) Stranger Things is vague about the history of Hopper and Joyce but David Harbour thinks they dated in high school.

(525) The Duffer Brothers didn't initially plan to show much of the Upside Down.

(526) A deal with Netflix to make Stranger Things only took 24 hours.

(527) Steve's red bandana in Stranger Things 2 is inspired by the red bandana worn by Josh Brolin in The Goonies.

(528) The Palace Arcade is located at 6501 Church St. in Douglasville.

(529) The Duffer Brothers pitched Montauk (aka Stranger Things) by creating a booklet that was designed to look like an old eighties paperback. The booklet had a story treatment and included photographs from some classic horror and fantasy movies to indicate the tone the show would be aiming for. The films that featured in the Montauk pitch booklet were E.T. the Extra-Terrestrial, Close Encounters of the Third Kind, Altered States, Poltergeist, Hellraiser, Stand By Me, Firestarter, A Nightmare On Elm Street, and Jaws.

(530) The location for the van flip sequence in season one was 3782 Sarah's Lane, in Tucker, GA.

(531) Gaten Matarazzo is considered to be the biggest prankster on the set of Stranger Things.

(532) Cary Elwes was always the first choice to play Mayor Kline.

(533) Dustin's "Lando" mantra in season one is a reference to the untrustworthy Lando Calrissian in The Empire Strikes Back.

(534) When they made season one, the cast had no idea if there would be a season two.

(535) The Duffer Brothers took inspiration from successful movie sequels in preparation for Stranger Things 2. They studied films like Temple of Doom, Aliens, Evil Dead II, and Terminator 2.

(536) In season one of Stranger Things, Holly Wheeler is dressed to look like Drew Barrymore's Gertie in E.T.

(537) Eleven's real name is Jane Ives. The birth certificate that Owens gives Hopper at the end of Stranger Things 2 has her name as Jane Ives Hopper.

(538)The Duffer Brothers had always wanted to create their own screen monster. The Demogorgon was the fulfilment of this dream.

(539) There have been a number of Stranger Things comics. These comics tend to be prequels or 'side stories' so that they don't clash with the actual TV show.

(540) The Duffer Brothers and Shawn Levy always suggest Dr Brenner is still alive. They say that if they had really killed him in season one they would have shown him die onscreen.

(541) Netflix were very 'hands off' when Stranger Things went into production. This gave the Duffer Brothers creative freedom - which was obviously an advantage to the show.

(542) Pez is an Austrian candy which comes in a dispenser.

(543) Netflix dubbed Stranger Things into nine languages and subtitled it in twenty-two. This made the show more accessible in international markets.

(544) Stone Mountain Park at 1000 Robert E. Lee Blvd. in Stone Mountain has been used for some exterior locations in Stranger Things. This was where, for example, Eleven looks at her reflection in the pond in season one.

(545) Because of the covid hiatus, Stranger Things 4 will be the first season of the show where the scripts were completed very early in the production.

(546) It is suggested in Stranger Things that Hopper used to be a cop in a big city.

(547) Millie Bobby Brown invented the little head flick Eleven sometimes does when she uses her powers.

(548) When Eleven watches All My Children on television in Stranger Things 2 she mimics the actress Susan Lucci.

(549) The Fury, a 1978 supernatural thriller directed by Brian De Palma, was an influence on Stranger Things. Adapted from the novel of the same name by its own author, John Farris, The Fury revolves around a secret area of the government's intelligence department trying to forge a division of super powered humans who have telekinesis.

(550) The sequence in The Spy where the soldiers entered the tunnels and are wiped out obviously owes much to the Colonial Marines coming off second best when they investigate the Xenomorph tunnels of the colony in James Cameron's Aliens.

(551) The Body takes its title from the Stephen King novella which was adapted into the classic Rob Reiner film Stand By

Me.

(552) The music in Stranger Things is heavily influenced by Tangerine Dream. Tangerine Dream is a German electronic music band formed in 1967 by Edgar Froese. They have composed many movie scores - including Legend, Near Dark, The Keep, Firestarter, and Risky Business.

(553) The horror prologue of the doomed scientist in the elevator in The Vanishing of Will Byers was inspired by a scene in Alien 3 where the alien creature pulls a victim up through the ceiling.

(554) Dr Brenner was called Agent One in the pitch for Montauk.

(555) Gaten Matarazzo said that he had never seen The Neverending Story before he had to sing the theme song for the Stranger Things 3 finale.

(556) Dustin's new invention in Stranger Things 3 is identical to Randall Peltzer's electric hammer in Joe Dante's Gremlins.

(557) Millie Bobby Brown won plaudits for a role in the BBC America series Intruders before Stranger Things. Stephen King singled her out for praise.

(558) In some of the early concept art for season one, the Demogorgon had a more humanoid looking face.

(559) David Harbour had never been a leading man in anything before he was cast in Stranger Things.

(560) Millie Bobby Brown was contemplating giving up on her acting aspirations before she auditioned for Stranger Things.

(561) Teaming up Steve with Dustin in Stranger Things 2 was not something that was planned from the start. They only had this idea two or three episodes into shooting.

(562) David Harbour said it was 'gross' cutting into the dummy of Will Byers in season one.

(563) The go ahead for season two was actually granted even before season one was released - such was the confidence that Netflix had in what they had seen so far.

(564) 3 Musketeers is a candy bar with whipped nougat made by Mars, Incorporated. This product was created in 1932. If you don't live in America, you might know this candy bar as a Milky Way.

(565) Matty Cardarople, who plays the Cheeto loving arcade and video store manager Keith, took a bag of Cheetos to his audition.

(566) Matty Cardarople has a spit bucket on the set so that he doesn't actually have to eat any Cheetos. It would probably be hard to act with your mouth full of Cheetos!

(567) Steve Harrington being given a truth serum by the Soviets in Stranger Things 3 is a homage to a scene in the James Cameron film True Lies.

(568) The password to enter Castle Byers is Radagast. Radagast is a wizard in Lord of the Rings.

(569) In the first season, Hopper tears his trailer home apart searching for a listening bug the lab might have planted. This is a homage to a similar scene in the Francis Ford Coppola film The Conversation.

(570) The child actor chosen to play Eleven had to have an expressive face and be able to express emotion without speaking. Millie Bobby Brown managed to tick all of these boxes.

(571) Dustin finds the school supply of Hunt's Snack Pack

chocolate puddings in the first season finale. In 1983 the puddings came in metal tins rather than plastic cups. The props department simply bought some metal tins of luncheon meat and put chocolate pudding labels on them.

(572) The make-up department on Stranger Things have sometimes used coffee granules to depict the muddied faces of those who have been exposed to the Upside Down.

(573) Charlie Heaton, who is English, had a lot of trouble saying Nancy in an American accent so he had to be dubbed whenever Jonathan says her name.

(574) During season one, Millie Bobby Brown turned up on the set one morning covered in gold glitter. It had to be removed before she could do any scenes.

(575) The driver who has his convertible taken by Hopper at the gas station in Stranger Things 3 is called 'Rich Douchebag Todd' in the credits.

(576) Dustin's quiff at the Snowball dance in Stranger Things 2 is inspired by Jon Cryer's "Duckie" Dale in the 1985 John Hughes film Pretty in Pink.

(577) We very briefly saw Bradford Haynes as Mr Sinclair in season one but Arnell Powell played this part in season two.

(578) 20% more users downloaded Netflix's mobile app in the third quarter of 2019. This coincided with the release of Stranger Things 3.

(579) Visual effects supervisor Paul Graff said there was a vague plan for a big monster sequence at the end of Stranger Things 3 which they decided not to shoot in the end.
"We heard this idea that the spider monster was going to crash the Fourth of July parade in Hawkins. It would be a real Godzilla-type story or like the T. Rex in Jurassic Park chasing the kids in a car. In my mind I was seeing shots of people

running away and screaming, and this mad panic. Maybe you'd see a tree getting knocked over or a car flying through the air and landing in the Hawkins movie theater. Maybe the Duffers would put the title of an '80s film they don't like on the marquee and we'd throw a car at it. I don't know — maybe that was a stupid idea."

(580) Mayor Kline is dressed like Michael Douglas as Gordon Gekko in Oliver Stone's 1987 film Wall Street in Stranger Things 3.

(581) The void of nothingness that Eleven enters in Stranger Things was influenced by Under the Skin. Under the Skin is 2013 film with Scarlett Johansson as an alien who preys on victims in a void of nothing with a liquid floor.

(582) There was a slight battle between Netflix and the Duffer Brothers on Stranger Things 2 when it came to swearing. Netflix wanted to do alternative takes of the scenes where the kids swear so that bad language was very minimal. The kids in the cast hated this idea because they thought scenes were much funnier with a few stray cuss words by their characters. The Duffers also preferred the takes with the odd cuss word so in the end Netflix conceded.

(583) You can see some 'Fraggles' as fairground prizes in Stranger Things 3. Fraggle Rock (1983-1987) was a children's television series created by Jim Henson.

(584) During the shooting of Bob Newby's death scene, Kate Trefry, a writer on Stranger Things, was the stand in for the DemoDog (which would be digitally added in later) that jumps on Bob.

(585) Some 3D printing was used to help design the look of the Demogorgon in season one.

(586) The Exorcist was a big influence on the possessed Will Byers story in Stranger Things 2.

(587) Francesca Reale, who plays the lifeguard Heather in Stranger Things 3, originally auditioned for the part of Robin Buckley.

(588) One of the things people find appealing about Stranger Things and the 1980s from a modern vantage point is that it depicts a time when our lives were not completely dominated by technology in the way that they are today.

(589) The Weirdo On Maple Street finds Dustin worrying that Eleven might be an escaped lunatic like Michael Myers. Michael Myers is the murderous antagonist of the Halloween film franchise. When the children go out trick or treating in Stranger Things 2, Max is dressed in a Michael Myers costume.

(590) Bob Newby talks to Joyce about moving to Maine in Stranger Things 2. Maine is the home of Stephen King.

(591) Charlie Heaton is a former rock band drummer.

(592) When Bob Newby restores the power to the lab in Stranger Things 2, Hopper quotes Jeff Goldblum in Jurassic Park by saying - "Son of a bitch did it!"

(593) The mousey hair of Joyce Byers in season one is said to be based on Meryl Streep in the film Silkwood.

(594) Reese's Pieces are a peanut butter candy product first introduced in 1977. Reese's Pieces became well known when they featured in the 1982 blockbuster film E.T. the Extra-Terrestrial. The sales of Reese's Pieces jumped by 85% after E.T. the Extra-Terrestrial was released.

(595) The Mall Rats is a title likely inspired by the 1995 Kevin Smith film Mallrats.

(596) The company Imaginary Forces created the title

sequence for Stranger Things. The Duffers rejected some of the first designs for looking too modern and generic.

(597) Wanna Fight from the Only god Forgives soundtrack by Cliff Martinez is patently the inspiration for the Stranger Things title theme.

(598) The Soviet baddie Grigori is clearly designed to evoke memories of Arnold Schwarzenegger in The Terminator.

(599) Eleven trying to move the train in The Lost Sister mirrors Luke Skywalker trying to raise the X-Wing from the swamp in The Empire Strikes Back.

(600) The smiley faced yellow yo-yo used by Jonathan and Nancy to set a trap for the Demogorgon in season one is a reference to the smiley face in Joe Dante's werewolf film The Howling.

(601) The very young children on the set of season one were told, to make them unafraid of it, that the Demogorgon was from Monsters Inc.

(602) The prehistoric bird picture that Eleven has on her wall in Stranger Things 3 was on the wall of the Wheeler basement in season one.

(603) Millie Bobby Brown said that Noah Schnapp had a comical mishap on the set of Stranger Things 2 when he got stuck in a chair. This was presumably during the sequence where Will Byers is tied down so that the Flayer can be burned from him.

(604) The Peterbilt truck in Dig Dug is a sly reference to the episode's director Andrew Stanton's Pixar film Cars.

(605) The beach scenes in Stranger Things 3 were shot in Malibu.

(606) The Mind Flayer was obviously one effect that couldn't be practical. The increased budget of season two (thanks to the huge success of season one) meant that more green screen work was required.

(607) When Dustin finds the chocolate pudding at the end of season one this is a nod to a similar moment 'Chunk' has in The Goonies.

(608) In the season one finale, Eleven kills some agents in a corridor and blood flows from their eyes. This gruesome touch is a homage to David Cronenberg's 1981 film Scanners.

(609) You can see someone dressed as Jason Vorhees (the hockey mask wearing killer from the Friday the 13th films) in the background when the kids are out trick or treating in Stranger Things 2.

(610) Benny's Burgers is really Tiffany's Kitchen in Lithia Springs, Georgia. This is a real diner that you can visit and eat in.

(611) Jonathan rents Mr Mom, Wargames, and Twilight Zone: The Movie from the VHS store in Stranger Things 2. Bob deciding to watch the movie Mr Mom at Halloween is a sly joke because Winona Ryder got her big break acting with Mr Mom star Michael Keaton in Tim Burton's Beetlejuice.

(612) The Triple-Decker Eggo Extravaganza that Hopper makes Eleven in Stranger Things 2 has whipped cream, Reese's Pieces, Hershey's Kisses, and jelly beans.

(613) The Duffer Brothers named The Bathtub as the season one episode they love the most. They enjoyed this episode because it brought all of the characters together for the first time.

(614) In the episode The Flayed, Grigori says to Hopper - "You're a policeman. Policemen have rules." This is a line a

terrorist says to John McClane in the original Die Hard.

(615) The prop master Lynda Reiss was the brains behind the 80s trappings that were crucial for the show. "I don't want to do a nostalgia-tinged product," said Reiss. "I want it to be the '80s. I don't want it to be what everyone just thinks is the '80s. Our baseline was the reality of the midwest in 1983."

(616) When he shot his death scene in Stranger Things 2, Sean Astin was chased down a corridor by a golf cart with a camera mounted on it.

(617) In the episode Will the Wise you can see a Kodak Movie Deck 425 Projector in the school classroom.

(618) Winona Ryder had no idea what streaming meant when she was told that Stranger Things would be on Netflix.

(619) Noah Schnapp and Winona Ryder begged the Duffer Brothers not to kill off Bob Newby because they loved working with Sean Astin.

(620) The band uniforms the Hawkins marching band wear in Stranger Things 3 were purchased from the Cheney Kansas High School.

(621) Mayor Kline's house in Stranger Things 3 was a real house the production team found.

(622) The make-up department gave Dacre Montgomery a few scars as Billy Hargrove because they thought Billy was the type of teenager who probably got into fights.

(623) The song playing at Will's funeral in season one is Elegia by New Order.

(624) In the pilot script for Montauk it is Lucas who has a crush on Mike's sister Nancy and not Dustin.

(625) Millie Bobby Brown said she did not enjoy having to eat strawberry ice-cream in Benny's diner in The Vanishing of Will Byers. "We were on set, and they asked what flavour I wanted. I told them I prefer light vanilla, but I asked what looks better on camera. Little things like that make a difference. They said strawberry. Ugh, that is my worst flavour. I asked the question, didn't I? So I was like OK. Fine. I ran to my trailer green. I wanted to vomit so badly."

(626) Randy Havens (Mr Clarke) had a mustache in real life when he went for his Stranger Things audition.

(627) Ross Duffer said - "It's scarier when you don't fully understand what's happening. If you were to encounter something from another world or dimension, it would be beyond comprehension."

(628) A 2010 film called Beyond the Black Rainbow is sometimes alleged to have influenced Stranger Things. Beyond the Black Rainbow is set in the 1980s and takes place at a mysterious lab where a young woman named Elena has psychic abilities.

(629) Bob Newby rents Twilight Zone: The Movie in Stranger Things 2. Twilight Zone: The Movie has a segment called It's A Good Life about a boy with terrifying psychic powers.

(630) Sarah, Will and Eleven are all seen with a cuddly lion toy at various points in Stranger Things. The significance or subtext of this remains unclear.

(631) Winona Ryder made her film debut in a movie called Lucas. It is plausible then that the first name of Lucas Sinclair is a Winona Ryder Easter egg.

(632) Hopper retrieving his hat in the Upside Down tunnels in Stranger Things 2 is obviously a homage to Indiana Jones.

(633) The Martian tripods from HG Wells' The War of the

Worlds were an influence on the Mind Flayer in season two.

(634) The Ghostbusters costume worn by Will Byers in season two is deliberately more homemade than that of the other boys.

(635) On the episode Trick or Treat, Freak, Natalia Dyer ended up with some punch on her cheek when Nancy gets drunk. They liked this detail and kept it in the episode.

(636) The World War 2 song We'll Meet Again (that we hear in Stranger Things 3) also appears in the Kubrick film Dr Strangelove.

(637) The character of Joyce Byers swears like a trooper in the Montauk pilot script but her language is considerably tamer in Stranger Things.

(638) The swoosh of the titles at the end of the Stranger Things title sequence was inspired by the film Bullit.

(639) The sets for the Soviet base in Stranger Things 3 are very Austin Powers - which in turn is a pastiche of the spectacular futuristic sets Ken Adam designed on the James Bond films.

(640) Alex P Keaton was the name of Michael J Fox's character in the popular eighties sitcom Family Ties. This is why Steve keeps referring to Marty McFly as Alex P Keaton in Stranger Things 3.

(641) Steve and Robin's costumes in Stranger Things 3 are similar to the pirate costumes from the Captain Hook Fish & Chip diner in the 1982 film Fast Times at Ridgemont High.

(642) The bus Eleven takes to Chicago to see Kali/Eight in The Lost Sister is the 422. 4 + 2 + 2 = 8.

(643) Eleven's hair in Stranger Things 2 was inspired by the cover of the 1981 book Ronja Rövardotter by Astrid Lindgren.

The cover in question features a girl with short curly hair in the woods.

(644) The Goonies is not showing at the Starcourt Mall cinema in Stranger Things 3. The Goonies opened about a month after Stranger Things 3 takes place.

(645) The 7-11 scene in Stranger Things 3 was shot near Tin Plate, down Milstead Ave in Conyers, Georgia.

(646) Bob Newby was originally going to be killed off much sooner in Stranger Things 2 but the Duffer Brothers were enjoying the performance of Sean Astin so they decided to keep him around for longer than planned.

(647) The first teaser trailer for Stranger Things 2 used a real 80s Eggo commercial featuring child actor Jason Hervey. Hervey later became well known for his role as Wayne Arnold in the comedy drama series The Wonder Years.

(648) During the bike chase in season one of Stranger Things, the boys shout out streets to head for and mention one named Elm.

(649) A telephone number is mentioned in Stranger Things 3 by Hopper when he is on the line with an operator. 618-625-8313. If you called this number after watching Stranger Things 3 you heard a message by Brett Gelman as Murray Bauman - "Hi! You have reached the residence of Murray Bauman. Mom, if this is you, please hang up and call me between the hours of 5 and 6 PM as previously discussed! Okay? And if this is Joyce, Joyce, thank you for calling, I've been trying to reach ya, I-I have an update. It's about, well it's uh... It's probably best if we speak in person, it's not good or bad, but it's... something. And if this is anyone but my mother or Joyce, well, you think you're real clever getting my number, don't you? Well here's some breaking news for you: You're not clever, you're not special, you're just one of the many, many nimwits to call here and the closest you will ever get to me is this prerecorded message! So,

after the beep, do me a favor. Hang up! And never call here again! You are a parasite! Thank you and good day!"

(650) David Harbour said that the 1985 Chevy Chase comedy film Fletch would be an influence on Stranger Things 3 but it's difficult to see too much evidence of this.

(651) The song playing when Nancy and Jonathan have breakfast in The Spy is Blue Bayou by Roy Orbison.

(652) E Pluribus Unum (Out of many, one) is a motto and appears on American money.

(653) The episode Dig Dug has a goof when Erica Sinclair uses Butterworth syrup on her french toast. Erica is using a plastic bottle but in 1984 this product came in glass bottles.

(654) Charlie Heaton did his audition for Stranger Things over the web in a London burger bar.

(655) Noah Schnapp was surprised to be cast in Stranger Things because he didn't think he did very well in his audition.

(656) Eleven displays recognition when she looks at a photograph of Will Byers in The Weirdo On Maple Street. This shot was inspired by a scene Peter Weir's Witness when the little amish boy (played by Lukas Haas) recognises a photograph in the police station.

(657) Billy's hair in Stranger Things 3 is a wig. Dacre Montgomery had short hair in real life at the time.

(658) When Karen explains to Billy in Stranger Things 3 why she didn't turn up to their secret meeting, Billy is holding some dangerous chemicals. This is a visual clue that Billy is now infected.

(659) Lucas Sinclair was named Lucas Conley in the pitch booklet for Montauk.

(660) TIME magazine said of Stranger Things 3 that - 'The more permanent paradigm shifts of this season not only offer audiences a number of powerful dramatic moments, but it also sets the stage for an entirely new dynamic in whatever comes next while also concluding this journey in a fulfilling way that doesn't actually require another season. After having spent three years with these characters, these revelations feel fully earned, all while reminding both the audience and the characters that you can never go back to merely sitting in your basement playing D&D, no matter how much joy that would bring you.'

(661) The Duffer Brothers have said Akira was an influence on Stranger Things. Akira is a 1988 Japanese animated film based on a comic. Akira is set in a future Tokyo and features psychics, telepathy, telekinesis, and secret government labs.

(662) Joe Keery auditioned for the part of Jonathan Byers before he was cast as Steve Harrington.

(663) Forty realistic stores were added to Gwinnett Place Mall for the Starcourt scenes in Stranger Things 3.

(664) The car on display in the Starcourt Mall is a 1985 Chrysler Lebaron Convertible.

(665) The tube of Pringles shown in Dustins's 'Mirkwood' food package in season one is a goof as this tube is actually from 1968.

(666) The Ghostbusters costumes worn by the boys in season two were fashioned from mechanic overalls.

(667) The undulating walls of the Byers house in season one feel inspired by the elasticity of television screens and flesh in David Croneberg's Videodrome.

(668) On his social media, Stephen King wrote of season one -

"Watching STRANGER THINGS is like watching Steve King's Greatest Hits. I mean that in a good way. STRANGER THINGS is pure fun. A+. Don't miss it. Winona Ryder shines."

(669) David Harbour thinks The Battle of Starcourt is the best Stranger Things episode ever made.

(670) In the season two episode The Spy, a soldier says "Stay frosty..." This is a line said by Michael Biehn's Hicks in the classic sequel Aliens.

(671) Eggo waffles were invented by Tony, Sam, and Frank Dorsa in California in 1953. We should point out that they merely invented the Eggo brand. Waffles and pancakes had been eaten in Europe for several centuries before they were introduced to America.

(672) The designer Eric Demeusy said of working on the Stranger Things title sequence - "I think with any title sequence it's important to set the tone and in this case it's mystery and suspense. So we start with the letters really big to the point where you don't really know what they are at first. As it progresses you start to realize they are letters and that they are the letters that make up the title. The show in a way is about putting the puzzle pieces together and metaphorically we used the type to do the same thing."

(673) The school bullies Troy and James never returned to the show after the first season.

(674) The word 'telekinesis' was first used in 1890 by Russian psychical researcher Alexander N. Aksakof.

(675) Steven Spielberg has praised Stranger Things and said he enjoys the show.

(676) It was the music of Michael Stein and Kyle Dixon in the independent film The Guest which brought them onto the radar of the Duffer Brothers.

(677) The Duffer Brothers seemed to suggest at times that Kali would be in Stranger Things 3 but she wasn't in the end.

(678) The cinema in Hawkins is screening The Terminator in Stranger Things 2.

(679) When the teenagers are trapped in the Gap store in the finale of Stranger Things 3, there are camera shots which homage Steven Spielberg's The War of the Worlds.

(680) Joe Keery said the only part of his Scoops Ahoy uniform he liked was the hat.

(681) When they began making season one of Stranger Things, the cast were not given all of the scripts and so didn't know how the story was going to end.

(682) The passage from Anne of Green Gables that Hopper reads to Eleven is - "I would feel so sad if I was a disappointment to her -- because she didn't live very long after that, you see. She died of a fever when I was just three months old. I do wish she'd lived long enough for me to remember calling her mother. I think it would be so sweet to say 'mother,' don't you? And father died four days afterwards from fever too. That left me an orphan and folks were at their wits' end, so Mrs. Thomas said, what to do with me. You see, nobody wanted me even then. It seems to be my fate."

(683) O'Bannon is the name of the state trooper who is part of the conspiracy to stop Will's body being examined in season one. O'Bannon is a reference to Dan O'Bannon, who wrote Alien and directed 1985's Return of the Living Dead.

(684) Winona Ryder said she has own back story for Joyce. She thinks Joyce was probably a sixties hippie.

(685) Peggy Miley, who plays Mrs Driscoll in Stranger Things 3, had never heard of Stranger Things before she was cast.

(686) Steve Harrington has some Nike Cortez. These sneakers were worn by Tom Hanks as Forrest Gump.

(687) Stranger Things has some similarities to Paper Girls - a comic by Brian K Vaughan that began in 2015. Paper Girls is set in 1988 and is about four girls who live in a small Cleveland town. While out on their morning paper round on bikes, they stumble into a perplexing science fiction mystery that launches them into alternate realities and the past and future.

(688) Stranger Things 2 saw a notable decrease in dialogue given to Mike, Nancy and Jonathan. These characters had (respectively) 199, 163, and 146 less lines in season two than in season one.

(689) Nancy goes a party at a girl named Tina's house in Stranger Things 2. In Wes Craven's A Nightmare On Elm Street, the central character Nancy had a best friend named Tina.

(690) The boys in Stranger Things use Telex Headsets on the ham radio.

(691) The Duffer Brothers had to promise Netflix that the spectacular stunt in season one where Eleven flips the van in the air would feature in the trailer.

(692) Dustin adopting a creature from the Upside Down was one of the first ideas the Duffer Brothers had for Stranger Things 2.

(693) The kids in the Stranger Things cast think that Gwinnett Place Mall is haunted.

(694) The school bully Troy's full name is Troy Walsh according to the Hawkins year book.

(695) The Sharp brand cash register at Scoops Ahoy is a

mistake because this model is from the 2000s.

(696) The basketball scene with Steve and Billy in Stranger Things 2 is a homage of a scene in Michael J Fox's eighties comedy film Teen Wolf.

(697) You can see a poster for the film version of Stephen King's Firestarter in Keith's video store at the end of Stranger Things 3.

(698) Steve Harrington and his friends shotgun beer in season one like John Cusack and Daphne Zuniga in Rob Reiner's 1983 film The Sure Thing.

(699) Walkie-talkies were popular with kids in the eighties, even if they were just talking to each other in the same house from upstairs! They were fun to use.

(700) When the boys and Eleven walk the train tracks in the woods during season one, these scenes deliberately evoke the Rob Reiner film Stand By Me.

(701) In the initial story treatment for Montauk, Jonathan and Nancy were going to become a couple much sooner than they do in Stranger Things.

(702) We see a Demogorgon egg in season one but this is never explained or expanded upon.

(703) Lucas wears clothes inspired by the 1984 film The Karate Kid in Stranger Things 3.

(704) The dimensional rift story in season one has many influences but perhaps the most obvious one is Stephen King's novella The Mist (which was later turned into a decent film by Frank Darabont). The story in The Mist has a town engulfed in a strange monster laden mist after a military experiment goes wrong.

(705) The creepy barn in Stranger Things 3 is owned by the Hess family. This is a reference to M. Night Shyamalan's 2002 film Signs.

(706) Andrew Stanton, when he directed the season two episode The Spy, set up a shot of Joyce walking into a conference room as a homage to a shot in the 1976 satirical comedy film Network.

(707) The Demogorgon has some obvious physical similarities with the Imps in the Doom video game series.

(708) On the 30th of September, 2019, a short teaser announcing Stranger Things 4 was released.

(709) Sadie Sink had five 'call backs' and an audition before she was cast as Maxine Mayfield for Stranger Things 2. This all took place in the space of two weeks.

(710) Bob Newby having a Dracula costume at Halloween in Stranger Things 2 is a light-hearted Easter egg. Winona Ryder starred in Francis Ford Coppola's version of Dracula in the early nineties.

(711) Mind Flayers are Illithids in Dungeons & Dragons. 'Illithids have a humanoid body with an octopus-like head,' write Dungeons & Dragons Wiki. 'They have four tentacles around a lamprey-like mouth, and require the brains of sentient creatures as part of their diet. An illithid who snares a living creature in all four of its tentacles can extract and devour its living brain. Their eyes are pale white, and they can see perfectly well in both darkness and light. Their sense of hearing is slightly poorer than a human's; they have difficulty distinguishing between several sounds mixed together, yet they are good at discerning from what direction sounds came from. Their skin is purplish blue to gray-green and covered in mucus, and is very sensitive to sunlight. They loathe sunlight, though it does not actually harm them. One of their most feared powers is the dreaded Mind Blast, where the illithid

emits a cone-shaped psionic shock wave with its mind in order to incapacitate any creature for a short amount of time. Illithids also have other psionic powers, generally telepathic in nature, although their exact effects have varied over editions. Other powers include a defensive psionic shield and powers of psionic domination for controlling the minds of others.'

(712) The Heathkitt ham radio belonging to Mr Clarke that the boys and Eleven use in season one to try and contact Will is a Heathkit DX-60. The term 'ham' means 'amateur' as in amateur radio.

(713) When Eleven searches under the floorboards of Hopper's cabin in season two, you catch a glimpse of a box marked Vietnam.

(714) Millie Bobby Brown and her family didn't really know what Eggo waffles were before Stranger Things.

(715) In Stranger Things 2, Paul Reiser's Dr Owens is introduced just as Carter Burke was in Aliens. Both are by a hospital bed and asking the patient to trust them.

(716) Mike Wheeler has a birthmark in the Montauk pilot script which the bullies make fun of and Mike also has a crush on Jennifer Hays.

(717) Noah Schnapp was away at Summer Camp when the Duffer Brothers telephoned him to say he had got the part of Will Byers.

(718) Although the cover of the book Ronja Rövardotter by Astrid Lindgren was cited as the main influence for Eleven's hair in Stranger Things 2, one might argue that she also has a similar hairstyle to the one Sigourney Weaver had in Aliens. Stranger Things 2 is rife with Aliens references so this might not be a coincidence.

(719) Mr Clarke is at home listening to My Bologna by Weird

Al Yankovic when he is visited by Joyce in Stranger Things 3. This song is a spoof of My Sharona by The Knack. My Sharona was used in the 1994 film Reality Bites - a film that had Winona Ryder and Ethan Hawke (Maya Hawke's father) as the leads.

(720) Deadline wrote of season one - 'Stranger Things is nothing if not a surprising, sometimes scary, moving and successful homage to the era of Spielberg's ET and the 1980s themselves, as well as the films of the great John Carpenter. Yes, there are a lot of clichés in Stranger Things, but like outdoor string lights, they all hold together. They also cast a warm glow on the sheer enthusiasm and respect the series has for those who have come before and a very particular time in America's recent history that now feels so far and so close at the same time.'

(721) When Will tells Joyce he isn't frightened of horror movies in season one, she replies "Oh yeah? Not even of... clowns?" This is obviously a reference to Pennywise from Stephen King's IT.

(722) Shawn Levy said that they considered fifty alternative songs for the Stranger Things 2 trailer before deciding that they simply had to get the rights to Michael Jackson's Thriller.

(723) Clive Barker's 1987 film Hellraiser was an influence on the special effects design in season one of Stranger Things. The Duffer Brothers liked the way that Hellraiser used practical effects for some very atmospheric and gruesome sequences. Obviously, Clive Barker didn't really have much choice at the time. He made Hellraiser on a modest budget and at a time when computer generated effects were still in their infancy.

(724) The Clash song Should I Stay or Should I Go is used a lot in season one as a commentary on the plight of poor Will. The song has a deeper meaning too in the show as it is a symbol of the bond between Will and Jonathan.

(725) At the Halloween party in Stranger Things 2, Nancy and Steve are dressed as Tom Cruise and Rebecca De Mornay in Risky Business.

(726) Bob Newby's death includes some little Easter eggs. When Hopper stops Joyce and says 'he's gone', this is a little homage to Drake's death in Aliens where Hicks says the same line to Vasquez. When Hopper pulls Joyce away after Bob's death, this feels a lot like the moment where where Aragorn pulls Frodo away after Gandalf dies in Lord of the Rings.

(727) The Duffer Brothers are just about old enough to have some memories of the 1980s themselves.

(728) David Harbour as Hopper has the most lines of the cast in season three. Harbour has 353 lines in Stranger Things 3.

(729) Mr Clarke watches John Carpenter's The Thing at home in season one despite the fact that the film hadn't been released on VHS yet as a rental at the time.

(730) Paul Reiser said that when he started shooting Stranger Things 2 he only had a few scripts and so had no idea if Dr Owens was going to turn out to be good or a villain.

(731) Dustin names portable radio tower Cerebro in Stranger Things 3 in tribute to Professor X.

(732) Stranger Things production designer Chris Trujillo said that Atalanta was chosen as the production base because the area had a very 'Anytown USA' quality. "Before deciding on Atlanta as our filming location, we were beset by the slightly overwhelming options of an open map. We talked about and explored everywhere from New England to coastal Carolina, from sunburnt Texas to the Pacific Northwest, but then it occurred to us that the world we wanted to create should be ubiquitous, instantly familiar to everyone; Anytown, USA. Suddenly, Atlanta was an obvious choice. It served us so well because Atlanta proper and the various towns that surround it

really represent a broad spectrum of archetypal Americana. There are all of these incredible neighborhoods, that, with very little modification, perfectly paint the picture of split-level ranch-style suburbia, born in the 60s, that came to define the look of 70s and 80s American life. So, we get rid of the DirecTV dishes, manicure the lawns, switch out a few mailboxes, fill the driveways with period correct station wagons and sedans and voila! You're ready to travel back in time with some misfit middle schoolers on BMX bikes."

(733) The special effects team built some animatronic rat models for Stranger Things 3 but these were discarded because they didn't seem convincing enough.

(734) Shooting on season two wrapped on June the 3rd 2017.

(735) Andrei Tarkovsky's 1979 science fiction film Stalker was an influence on the concept and design of the Upside Down. Stalker is about an expedition to a mysterious forbidden area called the Zone.

(736) At the Halloween party in Stranger Things 2, characters are dressed as (amongst others) John Belushi in Animal House, Madonna, Flashdance, Rocky, Siouxsie Sioux, and characters from The Karate Kid.

(737) When Suzie makes contact in The Battle of Starcourt, you can see Dustin's red, white, and blue hat from the first two seasons of Stranger Things in her bedroom.

(738) The broadcast Dustin intercepts in Stranger Things 3 plays Daisy Bell from 2001: A Space Odyssey.

(739) When Eleven wears a bandana blindfold to make contact with Mike through the static of the television in Stranger Things 2, this is a reference to The Karate Kid.

(740) Steve Harrington wears, among other things, a vintage Le Tigre polo shirt in season one.

(741) The location for the abandoned Steel Works in Stranger Things 3 was 2903 RN Martin Street East Point, GA.

(742) The first full trailer for Stranger Things 3 had 22 million views in one week on YouTube.

(743) When Mike Wheeler shouts "It's a trap!" in Stranger Things 2, he is quoting Admiral Ackbar in Return of the Jedi.

(744) Eleven has a Sharp QT-50 pastel boombox in season three.

(745) Joyce struggling with two machine keys in the season three finale is a homage to Richard Pryor doing a similar thing as Gus Gorman in Superman III.

(746) The Lost Sister is the lowest rated episode of Stranger Things on IMDB by some distance.

(747) Dustin's bike in season one has two different colours. The props department thought Dustin was probably the sort of kid who would start painting his bike but then get distracted by something and never finish this task.

(748) The Starcourt Mall cinema in Stranger Things 3 is showing or promoting The Stuff, Lifeforce, Fletch, Return to Oz, DARYL, Cocoon, Weird Science, Back to the Future, Day of the Dead, and The Black Cauldron.

(749) Hopper's tropical shirt in season three is inspired by Tom Selleck's casual wardrobe on the eighties private investigator action mystery show Magnum.

(750) During the production of Stranger Things 2, a fan infiltrated the set and got a photograph taken with Millie Bobby Brown.

(751) Shannon Purser said she found it quite moving to watch

Barb's funeral scene in Stranger Things 2.

(752) A deleted scene in season one had Eleven, while exploring the Wheeler house, reading Nancy's diary.

(753) Because so many bikes were needed (each of the stunt doubles for the children also had to have a bike) in season one, the bikes in the show are hybrids of different parts (mostly BMX) to create the appearance of early 80s bikes.

(754) The basketball scenes in Stranger Things 2 use the song Push IT to the Limit - which was from the soundtrack of Al Pacino's Scarface.

(755) The Scoop Troop (the team of Steve, Robin, Erica, and Dustin) in Stranger Things 3 was not something that was planned far in advance. Stranger Things producer and director Shawn Levy said that it just struck them one day that teaming up Erica with Steve and Dustin was potentially an amusing concept.

(756) Tangerine Dream often include their own version of the Stranger Things theme in their live sets.

(757) Max drives a car in Stranger Things 2 but is too short to use the pedals - just like Short Round in Indiana Jones and the Temple of Doom.

(758) Dustin proposes the Soviets might be experimenting in Promethium in their underground base in Stranger Things 3. Promethium was the substance used to create Cyborg in DC Comics.

(759) Linnea Berthelsen had never watched Stranger Things before when she was asked to audition for the part of Kali in Stranger Things 2. She binged the first season before the audition but it didn't prove to much help because they didn't tell her anything about the character or what Kali's role would be. She still got the part though.

(760) Waitresses at the Stranger Things 2 premiere were dressed in special Eggo yellow uniforms.

(761) The Soviet prison at the end of season three is set on the Kamchatka Peninsula, a Soviet peninsula located in Russia, across the Bering Strait from Alaska and within Siberia on the Pacific Coast.

(762) The Snowball dance at the end of Stranger Things 2 clearly takes some inspiration from the Enchantment Under the Sea dance in Back to the Future.

(763) Stephen King's Firestarter is a very obvious influence on Stranger Things. This story is about a young girl named Charlie with pyrokinetic powers as a result of her parents participating in MKUltra style experiments. This book was made into a 1984 film with a very young Drew Barrymore. Charlie's powers induce nosebeeds and she wears electronic equipment on her head in laboratory experiments.

(764) The hairstylist on Stranger Things said that Millie Bobby Brown kept losing the blonde wig that Eleven wears in season one. "One time, she was so sick of the blonde wig, I found it hanging on a tree branch, hanging in the wind."

(765) John Carpenter is clearly a big influence on Stranger Things, both in terms of his music and his movies. His 1984 film Starman is often overlooked in Stranger Things inspirations but it does have quite a lot in common with Spielberg's E.T and the way the character of Eleven is written and developed in Stranger Things.

(766) Noah Schnapp initially auditioned for the part of Mike Wheeler.

(767) Dustin is wearing a Castroville Artichoke Festival T-shirt near the end of season one.

(768) In season two, we see Karen Wheeler using a polaroid One Step Flash Camera. These types of cameras were a novelty in the eighties because you didn't have to take your photographs away to be developed.

(769) The cinema in Hawkins is screening the Tom Cruise film All the Right Moves in season one.

(770) There is a poster for the album Filth Hounds of Hades by Tank in Billy's room in Stranger Things 3.

(771) Matthew Modine said he was quite shocked by the glee of Millie Bobby Brown at shooting the scenes in season one where Eleven kills government agents.

(772) The Duffer Brothers said that Dr Brenner was one of the most difficult characters to write because he is very aloof and guarded.

(773) The Duffer Brothers said of Stranger Things - "We were pretty ordinary kids growing up in the suburbs of North Carolina, and when we watched films and read books, it made us feel like our rather normal lives had the potential for adventure. Maybe tomorrow we would find a treasure map in the attic, or maybe one of us would vanish into the television screen, or maybe there was a clown in that sewer grate down the street. The feeling was powerful and inspiring. There was nothing better. We wanted to capture that feeling again with Stranger Things."

(774) David Harbour says he was somewhat disillusioned with his acting career before Stranger Things came along and that the show felt like a last chance for him. "Stranger Things felt like a last at bat for me, and I was like, If I'm going to do this, I'm really going to swing for the fences and put my whole soul into this thing. I had gotten to a place in Hollywood where I was playing fifth and sixth on the call sheet. It was good – I could make a living and could support a theatre career that allowed me to do more artistic kind of stuff, but I had really

given up on the idea that I would be able to tell stories that I really cared about in TV or film."

(775) Stranger Things 2 has the most obscure reference of all. "When Dustin's on the phone, pretending he's looking for the cat, he's talking to Mr McCorkle," said Matt Duffer. "Mr McCorkle is our neighbor growing up. That's deep cut; you have to live in our neighborhood to know that one."

(776) The Duffer Brothers estimate that they had around fifteen rejections before signing a deal with Netflix to make Stranger Things.

(777) The death throes of Bob Newby are a homage to the demise of Robert Shaw's shark hunter Quint in Jaws.

(778) Matt Duffer said the video game Dark Souls was a big influence on Stranger Things. "We're huge, huge fans of the Dark Souls games, and there's something about when you're playing Dark Souls. Immediately when you're in that world, it was to do with the imagery, it has to do with the sound design, and you're just immediately very uncomfortable and on edge. We wanted you to feel that way when you're in the Upside Down."

(779) David Harbour said he found it difficult at first on Stranger Things 2 to shoot confrontational scenes with Millie Bobby Brown but soon realised that Brown was more than capable of holding her own with him.

(780) Billy Hargrove is dressed like Jack Burton in John Carpenter's Big Trouble in Little China at the end of Stranger Things 3.

(781) Barb's death scene was no picnic for Shannon Purser. She was covered in slime and had crew members yanking her ankles to depict the monster trying to drag her into the swimming pool.

(782) A 1993 X-Files episode called Eve is often alleged to have been an influence on Stranger Things. The story has Mulder and Scully discovering a secret government project that involves children. The children are numbered - with the main kids for the episode named Eve 9 and Eve 10.

(783) The Duffer Brothers worked on M. Night Shyamalan's mystery show Wayward Pines before they made Stranger Things. It taught them a lot about working in television.

(784) When Eleven eats the burger at Benny's Burgers in The Vanishing of Will Byers, Millie Bobby Brown had a spit bucket so that she didn't have to eat too much during the takes.

(785) Millie Bobby Brown said Eleven eating the fries at Benny's diner in The Vanishing of Will Byers was pretty awful to shoot because the fries were cold.

(786) It took five months to film the first season of Stranger Things.

(787) There is a poster for The Wizard of Oz in Suzie's bedroom in the finale of Stranger Things 3.

(788) Production designer Chris Trujillo, who had to design Starcourt Mall, worked in some malls when he was a teenager. This experience was something he drew on with Starcourt.

(789) Lucas wears a pair of Converse Fastbreak sneakers in Stranger Things 3.

(790) The overhead view of Joyce driving Will to the Hawkins Lab for a medical examination in Stranger Things 2 deliberately evokes the beginning of Stanley Kubrick's adaptation of Stephen King's The Shining. The start of Kubrick's film has overhead shots of Jack Nicholson and his family driving to the Overlook Hotel along mountain roads.

(791) Ice had to be imported to Atlanta to depict the frosty

Christmas weather in Hawkins at the end of season one.

(792) In the first episode of season two, MADMAX, Mike is sorting out some of his old toys to give away and becomes reflective when he picks up a dinosaur toy. This is because that was the toy he first showed Eleven when she lived in his basement in season one.

(793) The fairground scenes in Stranger Things 3 involving Hopper are patently inspired by the 2014 thriller film The Guest. At the end of The Guest, Dan Stevens is an apparently unstoppable antagonist doggedly pursuing his quarry through a neon carnival.

(794) Some of the music from Midnight Run is heard when Hopper and Joyce are on the road in season three. Midnight Run is a 1988 action comedy film with Robert De Niro.

(795) The Duffer Brothers have said that the 2013 post-apocalyptic video game the Last of Us was an influence on Stranger Things. This game has a character named Ellie.

(796) Mike Wheeler has a poster for Jim Henson's eighties fantasy film The Dark Crystal on his wall in season one.

(797) Dragon's Lair and Dig Dug were chosen for the Palace Arcade because (rather like Dungeons & Dragons in season one) they anticipated some of the plot of season two. "We were hoping to do with the arcade what we did in season one with D&D," said Ross Duffer, "which was to do a bit of foreshadowing for the whole season, with Lucas getting Princess Daphne, and the monsters in Dig Dug. We were hoping to roughly set up where we were going to go in the next nine hours."

(798) The Mind Flayer in season two seems to be inspired by Louise Bourgeois' spider like sculpture Maman.

(799) The props department wanted Mike Wheeler to wear an

E.T. watch in season one but it was too expensive to gain the rights.

(800) Sadie Sink said that, unlike her character Max Mayfield, she was terrible at the games in the Palace Arcade.

(801) Kali is the name of the god the thugee cult worship in Indiana Jones and the Temple of Doom.

(802) Hopper threatens to cut Mayor Kline's finger off with a cigar cutter in Stranger Things 3 like the villain in Sam Raimi's Darkman.

(803) Will's terrifying encounter with the Mind Flayer when he wanders to the door of his house at night in Stranger Things 2 is patently a homage to Spielberg's Close Encounters of the Third Kind.

(804) Den of Geek wrote of Stranger Things 2 - 'Fans only want to know one thing when searching for a spoiler-free review like this one. Is Stranger Things season 2 as good as or better than the first run? The truth is nothing could equal the sense of discovery and nostalgia that the first season captured, but this new instalment beautifully expands upon the existing tale, adding a few additional characters and answering some lingering questions. Although Will somewhat supplants Mike as the emotional core of the show, the existence of parallel storylines, including both familiar pairings and unexpected allies, reminds us of the best storytelling from season one.'

(805) The void sequences featuring Eleven in Stranger Things 3 were slightly more elaborate than in previous seasons. They were shot in a square shaped shallow pool on a soundstage with black surroundings.

(806) The scenes of the Mind Flayer lurking around the Byers house in season two are a homage to The Evil Dead.

(807) Gaten Matarazzo has improvised a few lines as Dustin

that were kept in the show because the Duffer Brothers enjoyed them.

(808) Although season one included some practical effects, by the time of Stranger Things 3 the special effects were purely digital. This was an unavoidable consequence of the special effects becoming larger in scope and more complex.

(809) In their interviews for Stranger Things 2, the Duffers said that Millie Bobby Brown was always game to do multiple takes of a scene to make it absolutely perfect.

(810) Dustin's pet creature Dart was complex to design because Dart had to go through four stages of development from slug to Deomodog.

(811) The Lost Sister has some graffiti in the background which is an Easter egg for Grant Morrison's comic The Invisibles.

(812) In Stranger Things 3, Dustin has been to Camp Know Where. Camp Nowhere is the name of a 1994 film with Christopher Lloyd.

(813) Hopper has a IBM Selectric III typewriter in his police office.

(814) The 1978 remake of Invasion of the Body Snatchers was an influence on the organic plant fungi look of the Demogorgon and Upside Down.

(815) Officers Powell and Callahan are patterned on the paranormal investigator's assistants in Poltergeist.

(816) The kids in the Stranger Things cast like to have their trailers near one another on the set.

(817) Kali's gang are said to be inspired by Walter Hill's film The Warriors.

(818) A game called Quest for the Space Knife is seen in the Palace Arcade. This is a fictitious game and a reference to one of the production crew of Stranger Things having a music group called Space Knife. A poster for a movie called Quest for the Space Knife can be seen in the cinema lobby in season two.

(819) In the pilot script for Montauk (as the show was called at first), Benny's second named is Henderson. This seems to indicate that Benny was initially conceived as a relative to Dustin.

(820) There is evidence that LSD MkUltra experiments took place at Camp Hero. Some rooms in the derelict base with psychedelic wallpaper were found. However, the other Montauk conspiracy theories like teleportation, time travel, and aliens, are purely fictional.

(821) The kids in the show are alleged to have earned $20,000 an episode in season one. By the time of season three, they were alleged to be on $250,000 an episode.

(822) Will Byers has some copies of Dragon magazine at Castle Byers. This was a magazine for Dungeons & Dragons fans.

(823) Maya Hawke as Robin says the line in "I'll take those odds" in Stranger Things 3. This is a line Maya Hawke's father Ethan Hawke said in the film Gattaca.

(824) Stein and Dixon said that one of the potential pitfalls of a synth score is that it can sound cheesy if it isn't done right. They were very conscious of avoiding this when they composed the music for Stranger Things.

(825) Some of the theme from Joe Dante's film Gremlins soundtrack can be heard when Dart is loose at the school in Stranger Things 2.

(826) Dacre Montgomery said the Duffer Brothers told him that Billy Hargrove was inspired by the possessed writer Jake Torrance in The Shining.

(827) Jonathan and Nancy play out a flirtatious bedroom farce at Murray's house in Stranger Things 2. This is a homage to Harrison Ford and Kate Capshaw in the palace scenes in Indiana Jones and the Temple of Doom.

(828) After the success of the first season of the show in 2016, the kids in the cast went out trick or treating but found that no one recognised them.

(829) The Mall Rats mentions telephone numbers in the 765 area code. In 1985 though it would have been area code 317 in Indiana.

(830) The Mind Flayer takes some inspiration from Lovecraft's cosmic entity Cthulhu.

(831) The Duffer Brothers originally planned for Mike and Eleven to be reunited at the Snowball dance in the finale of Stranger Things 2. The reunion took place though in the penultimate episode.

(832) Joe Keery hurt his back shooting the tense junkyard sequence in Stranger Things 2. "It's a real live set that was in this junkyard. It's a rough sort of thing to do because you're diving in this bus 30 times. I actually I landed on my back so I kind of screwed up my back a little bit."

(833) When we see a scientist explore the Upside Down on a safety winch in season one and meet a grisly demise, the scientist is called Shephard. Shephard, as we mentioned, is the name of a major character in the video game Silent Hill. It could be though that this character is a reference a character named Shepherd who appears in the 1984 horror film C.H.U.D. A third potential reference could be Alan Shepard -

who was the second American astronaut in space and part of the Apollo program.

(834) The Farrah Fawcett hair care spray that Steve Harrington likes was a real product by Fabergé Organics. However, it was discontinued in 1984.

(835) Stranger Things writer Kate Trefry was the person who suggested having a mall in Stranger Things 3.

(836) It is sometimes reported that Montauk was pitched as an anthology show but the evidence seems to contradict this. The pitch book for Montauk clearly proposed one single story and one set of characters.

(837) Kyle Lambert was shown a rough cut of the first two episodes of season two before he began designing his Stranger Things 2 poster.

(838) Shannon Purser said she was touched by the popularity of Barb. "It still blows me away that she (Barb) got the kind of response that she did. A lot of it, I think, is timing. I think a lot of people definitely relate to the people who are less than conventional - at least by Hollywood standards - people who are an outcast and awkward, because more often than not, we don't feel like the cool, popular kid who had everything together in high school. Most of us have been a third wheel or have been stuck at a party we didn't want to be at. I think there's definitely this fondness about Barb and her situation because we've all been there before."

(839) Dragon's Lair was not a conventional arcade game. You made a choice and then watched the animation play out and you see if your decision got Dirk Daring killed or not. As a consequence, the game didn't have long lasting appeal because you either learned the pattern (which required a lot of money and time) or simply grew frustrated at watching Dirk get killed for 50 cents a time.

(840) Dungeons & Dragons was heavily influenced by Tolkien.

(841) Production designer Chris Trujillo said the Hawkins Laboratory had to have a Cold War atmosphere. "It was important that Hawkins Laboratory feel like an imposing, threatening entity looming secretly in your backyard. In that way, it works as a physical reflection of the Reagan Era, residual Red Scare, Cold War anxiety that's lying just under the surface in Hawkins, Indiana."

(842) The Duffer Brothers said they didn't like Dragon's Lair very much themselves. "Dragon's Lair we played a lot as kids. It's a fun game to look at — it's not a very fun game to play. Everyone who played it as a kid had the same experience: It's outrageously expensive, it looks really cool, it draws you in like a magnet, and then it just takes your money and is very frustrating. All these barcades are popping up now, and I was at one recently and they had Dragon's Lair there. And no one is playing it because it's not a very good game. But it's still 50 cents! It's 2017 now, and 50 cents is a lot less, but it still felt like it was ripping you off. It's such an impossible game."

(843) In season one, Hopper has a Motorola walkie-talkie which is too modern for 1983.

(844) It needed 1,200 pounds of salt to make Eleven/Millie Bobby Brown float in the kiddie paddling pool for The Bathtub.

(845) The character of Kali was going to be called Roman before they changed the gender.

(846) The Duffer Brothers have never been involved in any 'side projects' alongside Stranger Things because they say they can only concentrate on one thing at a time.

(847) The story thread in Stranger Things 3 where Billy becomes possessed by the Flayer was originally supposed to be

in Stranger Things 2. They simply didn't have room for this plot arc in season two though.

(848) Sleepy Hollow Farm turned Hopper's cabin into a Stranger Things themed escape room where you could solve a mystery for $33.00.

(849) Joyce Byers' insistence that Will is alive was inspired by Richard Dreyfuss in Close Encounters of the Third Kind. The Dreyfuss character in Spielberg's film becomes very frazzled after a strange experience - just as Joyce does in season one of Stranger Things.

(850) The Hess farm mailbox being destroyed when Hopper and Joyce escape from Grigori in Stranger Things 3 is an Easter egg to Back to the Future where the mailbox at Peabody's farm is destroyed when Otis Peabody shoots at the DeLorean.

(851) David Harbour said it was his suggestion that Hopper should sacrifice himself in Stranger Things 3.

(852) Dustin references to the Griswold family in Stranger Things 3. National Lampoon's Vacation was a hit 1983 film featuring Chevy Chase as the accident prone head of the Griswold family. There were three sequels - European Vacation, Christmas Vacation, and Vegas Vacation.

(853) In the pitch booklet for Montauk, the Duffer Brothers say that the music in their show will be inspired by the scores for the John Carpenter films The Fog and The Thing.

(854) Despite his influence on Stranger Things, John Carpenter feels that the music in the show doesn't sound like his music at all.

(855) Millie Bobby Brown said she watched the Disney Channel to hone her American accent for Stranger Things.

(856) The slug that will coughs up at the end of season one was made of gummies and apple sauce. Noah Schnapp found this concoction revolting.

(857) The highest rated episode of season three on IMDB is The Battle of Starcourt with 9.3.

(858) Eleven wears a baby mask from Terry Gilliam's film Brazil in The Lost Sister.

(859) The set used as the Wheeler's home was also used in Scream: The TV Series.

(860) Dustin's pet DemoDog Dart has something of Ridley Scott's Alien in the manner that the creature sheds its skin and grows very rapidly.

(861) Eleven's ability to eat huge amounts of food in season one might be a reference to the DC Comics superhero The Flash. The Flash has to eat a lot of food to replenish the energy expended by the use of his powers.

(862) Noah Schnapp lost his voice for three days after shooting on Stranger Things 2 wrapped because he had done so much screaming.

(863) Shawn Levy said that there are surprisingly few deleted scenes in Stranger Things because the writing is very meticulous.

(864) The Clash were a British punk rock band who formed in 1976. Their song Should I Stay or Should I Go features heavily in season one.

(865) There are some croquet mallets in the Byers house in season one. This is a reference to the Winona Ryder film Heathers.

(866) Kyle Lambert said it is always a great thrill to see a

billboard with one of his Stranger Things posters.

(867) The use of flamethrowers on the Upside Down in Stranger Things 2 is evocative of John Carpenter's The Thing.

(868) Eleven encounters a fiery fantastical farm tornado in Stranger Things 3. This is a reference to Dorothy in The Wizard of Oz.

(869) The Dark Phoenix Saga by Chris Claremont and John Byrne (which collects together X-Men #129-137) was an influence on the character of Eleven and is referenced in season one. The story concerns the mutant superhero team facing a great crisis when the telekinetic Jean Grey is transformed into the all powerful Dark Phoenix.

(870) The very eagle-eyed will notice that among the films and posters in Keith's video store at the end of Stranger Things 3 are The Lonely Guy, Tank, 48 Hrs, The Flamingo Kid, National Lampoon's Vacation, Bachelor Party, Zapped!, Dead Men Don't Wear Plaid, Mad Max, Bustin' Loose, Car wash, Tron, Trading Places, Truck Turner, Five Deadly Venoms, D.C. Cab, The Man with Two Brains, The Incredible Shrinking Woman, The Jerk, Alone in the Dark, Mr Mom, Valley Girl, Supergirl, The Outsiders, Scarface, Sixteen Candles, Private School, and Fast times at Ridgemont high.

(871) Canada was where Stranger Things went viral the quickest.

(872) Dustin names the quest to find Will Byers in season one Operation Mirkwood. Mirkwood was a great forest in Tolkien's Middle-earth.

(873) The 2016 film X-Men: Apocalypse, which is set in the 1980s, has a deleted scene where the younger characters visit a mall which is drenched in neon, arcades, sneaker stores, lycra, and fast food. It seems very possible that the Duffer Brothers watched this scene before they made Stranger Things 3.

(874) Netflix was founded by by Reed Hastings and Marc Randolph in 1997 as a video rental company. Netflix only started producing their own content in 2013.

(875) There were no scripts yet when Winona Ryder agreed to play Joyce Byers. It was therefore something of a leap of faith on her part.

(876) Family Feud is seen on television in Stranger Things 2. Family Feud was a game show hosted by Richard Dawson. Dawson played the villainous game show presenter in the 1987 film (based on Stephen King's book) The Running Man.

(877) The scene where the teenagers push Dustin's radio tower aloft in Suzie, Do You Copy? mimics the World War 2 photograph where United States Marines raised the flag atop Mount Suribachi at the Battle of Iwo Jima.

(878) Robin sliding down the middle of the Starcourt Mall escalators is an Easter egg to George A Romero's Dawn of the Dead (where Scott Reiniger slid down the escalators in the Monroeville Mall).

(879) The fairground rides in Stranger Things 3 were supplied by the family owned company Forever Young Amusements

(880) Winona Ryder and Matthew Modine had known each for years before Stranger Things. They both appeared in the music video for Roy Orbison's A Love So Beautiful in the late 1980s.

(881) For kids in the early eighties, the video game arcade was still a thing of wonder that offered them a gaming experience they couldn't get on their machines at home.

(882) Joe Keery did a lot of swimming before season one because he was told that Steve Harrington was going to be the school swimming champion.

(883) Millie Bobby Brown as Eleven says only 246 words in season one of Stranger Things.

(884) Truesight is a Dungeons & Dragons spell to see the world as it actually is.

(885) Nancy uses a Sony Cassette Recorder in Dig Dug. Cassette tapes were widely used in the 1980s (and beyond).

(886) In Dungeons & Dragons, the Shadowfell (aka the Plane of Shadow) is a desolate reflection or echo realm.

(887) There is a scientific mistake regarding the Planck constant (a physical constant that is the quantum of electromagnetic action) in Stranger Things 3. Suzie gives Dustin the 2017 value of Planck's constant when, as this was 1985, she should have given him the 1973 value.

(888) The Palace Arcade in Stranger Things 2 is named after the 20 Grand Palace Arcade in the 1983 Cold War teen fantasy film WarGames.

(889) The Duffer Brothers were very impressed by the knowledge the kids in season one seemed to have of eighties movies.

(890) The song Higher and Higher by Jackie Wilson features in The Battle of Starcourt. This song was also used in the film Ghostbusters II.

(891) Charlie Heaton and Sadie Sink have both said that they don't like horror movies or horror shows in real life.

(892) The man who played the monster (before the digital effects were done in post-production) on the set in Stranger Things 3 was stunt coordinator Ken Barefield. Barefield had to wear a red spandex suit.

(893) Gaten Matarazzo said that he and the other younger cast members love night shoots most of all on Stranger Things.

(894) Jake Busey said he had no idea he was reading for Stranger Things 3 when he did his audition. He was a fan of the show though so it was all good.

(896) The casting of Winona Ryder happily mitigated any desire Netflix might have had to pursue better known actors for the other parts. This allowed the Duffers and their casting director to cast who they wanted - even if those people were complete unknowns who hadn't done anything else.

(897) Stranger Things producer and director Shawn Levy has a cameo as a coroner in The Body.

(898) When Joyce fails to turn up to her dinner date with Hopper in Stranger Things 3, a drunk Hopper says "I can do anything I want. I'm the chief of police." Roy Scheider (as Chief Brody) has this same line in Jaws.

(899) When Steve Harrington climbs up to Nancy's bedroom in season one, this is a homage to Wes Craven's Scream (where early on we see Neve Campbell's boyfriend do the same thing).

(900) Shawn Levy spent two months wrangling with the lawyers of the Michael Jackson estate to gain permission to use the song Thriller in the Stranger Things 2 trailer.

(901) Dacre Montgomery drew on his own experience of being bullied at school when he took on the role of Billy Hargrove.

(902) When Chief Hopper investigates the farm in the first episode of Stranger Things 2 we hear a few cues from the Predator score.

(903) The concept of a multiverse or alternate dimensions is not quite as fantastical as it sounds. Some scientists think they

could exist.

(904) The scene at the end of The Mind Flayer when Eleven returns feels rather like a homage to the scene in Alien Resurrection where Winona Ryder's android character Call is revealed again despite apparently just dying.

(905) Will plays the soundtrack to The Dark Crystal for his Dungeons & Dragons game in Stranger Things 3.

(906) The downtown store where Joyce works in Stranger Things 3 feels like part of a ghost town. This scene is designed to mimic the start of George A Romero's 1985 zombie film Day of the Dead where the characters encounter a deserted Florida town.

(907) The 1980 Ken Russell film Altered States features sensory deprivation experiments and was cited as a Stranger Things influence in the pitch booklet.

(908) Sadie Sink was nearly rejected in her first casting meeting because they thought she might be too tall. They had forgotten though that the other kids were a year older.

(909) The Lost Sister includes some music taken from a deleted a scene in the John Carpenter film Escape from New York.

(910) The TRC-214 walkie-talkies in season one (which takes place in 1983) didn't appear in RadioShack catalogues until 1985.

(911) When the Demogorgon battles the boys and Eleven at the end of season one this is a digital effect.

(912) In Stranger Things 2, there is a periodic table in the school containing elements that hadn't been discovered yet in 1984.

(913) Shannon Purser said they covered the set in glycerin and slime to shoot Barb's death scene in season one.

(914) The Pez dispenser Dustin has in season one is a bit of mistake because it is a 1999 container.

(915) Joe Keery and Noah Schnapp were upgraded to full recurring cast members for Stranger Things 2.

(916) Hopper promises Eleven he'll be home at 5:15 in Stranger Things 2. 5 + 1 + 5 = 11.

(917) Gabriella Pizzolo was a big fan of The Neverending Story even before being cast in Stranger Things 3.

(918) The containers of green gloop Steve's gang find in Stranger Things 3 resemble the Cryo-Can Embryo Vials in Jurassic Park.

(919) The makeup department smeared Dacre Montgomery in lipgloss during The Sauna Test to make Billy look hot and sweaty.

(920) The costume designers on Stranger Things said that old pictures of Rob Lowe were an influence on the look of Billy Hargrove. Billy has the same hairstyle that Rob Lowe had in the film St Elmo's Fire.

(921) The original episode titles for season two were Madmax, The Boy Who Came Back to Life, The Pumpkin Patch, The Palace, The Storm, The Pollywog, The Secret Cabin, The Brain, The Lost Brother. The Lost Brother is confirmation that Kali was originally going to be a male character.

(922) Joe Keery and Dacre Montgomery had to do a lot of basketball practice to prepare for the basketball scenes in Stranger Things 2.

(923) Gaten Matazarro said he was banned from sending his

brother texts during production on Stranger Things 2 because they were afraid to might let slip a spoiler.

(924) The scene in Stranger Things 3 where Karen Wheeler is about to go and meet Billy but then comes to her senses (when she sees Ted and Holly asleep in a chair) was suggested by Cara Buono.

(925) The Madonna song Material Girl plays over the Max and Eleven Starcourt Mall montage in Stranger Things 3. Madonna songs were also played on the set when they shot this sequence.

(926) Stranger Things 3 may have been influenced by Parasite Eve - a PS1-era RPG based on a novel by Hideaki Sena. Rats feature heavily in this game.

(927) Karen Wheeler is reading Johanna Lindsey's romance novel Heart of Thunder in the bath when Billy Hargrove knocks on her door in Stranger Things 2. The lovers on the cover of the book are illustrated to look like Karen and Billy.

(928) The scene near the end of Stranger Things 2 where Dr Owens offers Hopper half of his sandwich is a reference to the 1982 cult film Diner. In that film, Paul Reiser's character was always asking people if they were going to finish their sandwich.

(929) Eleven has a picture of Mike in his Ghostbusters costume on her bedside table in Stranger Things 3.

(930) Charlie Heaton punched Joe Keery a couple of times by accident when they shot the alley fight between Jonathan and Steve in season one.

(931) In 1992 Robert Redford film Sneakers a characters says - "It's fascinating what 50 bucks will get you at the county recorder's office. Playtronics Corporate Headquarters, the complete blueprints." In Stranger Things 3, Robin says - "It is

fascinating what 20 bucks will get you at the county recorders office. Starcourt Mall. The complete blueprints."

(932) Cary Elwes was already a fan of Stranger Things when he was cast as Mayor Kline.

(933) Ray Carrol, the former lab employee Kali is after in The Lost Sister, is watching Punky Brewster on television. Punky Brewster was a kids sitcom about a young girl being raised by a foster father. The show began in September 1984.

(934) The nightmares featuring Baldo the clown that Bob Newby speaks of in season two are another reference to Pennywise from Stephen King's IT.

(935) The Christmas lights that Joyce so famously deploys in season one are made by Santa-Trim.

(936) Glennellen Anderson, who plays Nicole in a couple of season one episodes, originally read for the part of Barb Holland.

(937) Dacre Montgomery put on some weight to play Billy Hargrove because he thought it wouldn't be realistic for an ordinary eighties teenager to have a 'shredded' Hollywood gym body.

(938) Noah Schnapp said that the first season was strange for him because, unlike the other cast members, he commuted to Atlanta from New York. It was only on season two (where Schnapp and his family were based in Atlanta like the others) where he felt like a main member of the cast.

(939) The twins who alternated as Holly Wheeler in season one had previously played baby Judith on The Walking Dead.

(940) The title of the Stranger Things 2 finale is a probable tribute to the 1987 horror fantasy film The Gate. The Gate is about two young boys who release a horde of demons through

a portal hole in their garden.

(941) Will Byers wears a Nelsonic Q-bert game watch in Stranger Things 3.

(942) The Upside Down in Stranger Things, especially in season one, might owe something to a 1964 Outer Limits episode called A Feasibility Study.

(943) The makeup department had to rough Dacre Montgomery up somewhat to turn him into Billy Hargrove. Montgomery was a bit too pretty as he was so they gave him a few cuts and scars and frizzed his hair up.

(944) Andrey Ivchenko, who plays the Terminator style Soviet baddie Grigori, was born in Ukraine when it was still part of the Soviet Union. He served in the Red Army for two years.

(945) Dustin has a Casio F-91W digital watch in Stranger Things 2. This is a mistake because these watches only came out in 1991.

(946) You can see an Annie wig in the store Joyce works in at the start of Stranger Things 2. Sadie Sink played Annie on the stage so this is probably a joke reference.

(947) The Chevrolet Caprice police cars seen in Stranger Things 2 have rectangular headlights which were not in use in 1984. It was only in 1987 that these headlights came into service.

(948) Sadie Sink had to do some skateboarding training for Stranger Things 2.

(949) In the news clip at the end of Stranger Things 3, a newspaper article by Caitlin Schneiderhan tells us that Hopper died in a fire. Caitlin Schneiderhan is an assistant to the Duffer Brothers.

(950) At the end of Stranger Things 3, Eleven is wearing the same shirt that she wears at the end of the first episode of Stranger Things 2.

(951) Eleven watches the 1931 film Frankenstein in the cabin in Stranger Things 2.

(952) Some younger fans of Stranger Things were said to be puzzled by the scenes of Jonathan developing photographs in the newspaper darkroom. They obviously didn't have iPhones in 1985 so that was how you developed photographs.

(953) Near the end of Stranger Things 3, Nancy shoots at Billy's speeding car in the same pose as Adrienne Barbeau shooting at the Duke's car in John Carpenter's Escape from New York.

(954) Dustin says his girlfriend Suzie is 'hotter' than Phoebe Cates in Stranger Things 3. Phoebe Cates is an actress best known for Fast Times at Ridgemont High and Gremlins.

(955) In the season two episode Trick or Treat, Freak, we see a flashback depicting how Eleven escaped from the Upside Down. By this time, Millie Bobby Brown's hair had grown considerably since season one so they had to use computer generated effects to recreate her season one buzzcut.

(956) The use of rats in Stranger Things 3 evokes Graveyard Shift - a short story by Stephen King.

(957) The Cold War was on its last legs in 1985 when Stranger Things 3 takes place. The Soviet Union would only last until 1990.

(958) On his social media, Stephen King wrote of season two of Stranger Things - "Ladies and gentlemen, that's how you do it. No bull****, balls to the wall entertainment. Straight up."

(959) The goo that Barb spits out in the swimming pool in her

death scene had to be syringed into Shannon Purser's mouth for each new take.

(960) Mike Wheeler has a calculator watch. These were popular in the 1980s.

(961) David Harbour said he binged the first season when it came out and was surprised at how emotional he found it. "I was on my couch in the East Village watching the scene where I'm saving Will and I'm crying on my couch. I forgot completely that it was me, that I was involved in the show."

(962) In the scene at the end of The Mind Flayer, where Eleven finally returns and sees Mike for the first time, Finn Wolfhard was not on the set that day so Millie Bobby Brown had to do Eleven's reaction shot (at seeing Mike) alone.

(963) In the first season finale we see in flashbacks that Sara Hopper is being treated in hospital. Jim Hopper is seen distraught on a hospital stairwell. The stairwell is later revealed to be identical to the one in the Hawkins Laboratory.

(964) Demogorgons featured in John Milton's Paradise Lost and Ludovico Ariosto's Orlando Furioso.

(965) Finn Wolfhard thinks Pennywise the clown from Stephen King's IT is scarier than the Demogorgon.

(966) Charlie Heaton isn't the biggest fan of The Clash - despite his character Jonathan Byers loving them.

(967) The Duffer Brothers say they decided to cast David Harbour as Jim Hopper after watching him in the 2014 WGN America show Manhattan. Manhattan was a short lived show about the American government project that created the first atomic weapons.

(968) Erica Sinclair has a drawing of a rainbow and a sunflower on her wall in Stranger Things 2. These are two of

the words that Terry Ives recites on a loop.

(969) Dacre Montgomery said the Duffer Brothers always allow the actors some creative input into their characters. "They are in an open forum with their actors, which provides everybody with an opportunity to evolve the character over a season rather than it being predetermined."

(970) Dustin's 'do you like these pearls?' growl in season two was based on Gaten Matarazzo's impression of Chewbacca from Star Wars.

(971) We see Steve find the Christmas lights from season one in Stranger Things 2.

(972) Natalia Dyer said she knew Stranger Things was a big hit when people started to recognise her in New York only hours after the show had started streaming for the first time.

(973) The Duffer Brothers said that Mr Clarke functions as the eighties version of Wikipedia in season one of Stranger Things. He is there to answer any science questions the boys might have.

(974) John Paul Reynolds, who plays Officer Callahan in Stranger Things, said that he is the only cast member who is never recognised or asked for an autograph.

(975) The M9s that the agents carry in season one did not become a military sidearm until 1985.

(976) Dustin's research in Stranger Things 2 suggests Indirana semipalmata as the species of frog Dart might be. However, Indirana semipalmata wasn't classified until 1986.

(977) Instances of babies being given the name Dustin went up by 30% in the twelve months after season one of Stranger Things was released.

(978) Cheers is shown on television in both seasons two and three of Stranger Things. Cheers was a classic NBC sitcom that ran from 1982 to 1993. It starred Ted Danson and was set in a Boston bar where everyone knows your name.

(979) Millie Bobby Brown's lucky number in real life is 8.

(980) At the end of The Mind Flayer, when everyone is preparing for a DemoDog onslaught on the cabin, Mike Wheeler has a candlestick as a weapon.

(981) Kyle Lambert did the sketching for his Stranger Things posters using Procreate on an iPad Pro with an Apple Pencil.

(982) Finn Wolfhard said the Dustin/Suzie Neverending Story song duet is the sequence he loves the most in Stranger Things.

(983) Hopper is called a Fat Rambo in Stranger Things 3. John Rambo is an action hero character played by Sylvester Stallone. Rambo: First Blood Part II was a big hit in 1985. It was a sequel to 1982's First Blood.

(984) Steve and Dustin are bemused by a Jazzercise class in Stranger Things 3. Jazzercise is a dance fitness workout.

(985) The kids hiding from the monster in Starcourt Mall in Stranger Things 3 is inspired by the children hiding from the raptors in Jurassic Park.

(986) It is apparent in the Christmas scenes at the end of season one that Joyce Byers has (understandably) decided not to put up any Christmas lights.

(987) Eleven doesn't eat any Eggos in season three.

(988) The Soviet security men use a Tokarev TT-33 pistol in Stranger Things 3.

(989) Dustin Henderson is the only one of the gang of boys in Stranger Things not to have any siblings.

(990) A DVD of season one by Target was designed so that the DVD looked like a faded VHS tape.

(991) David Harbour was initially worried that Stranger Things was going to bomb because he felt the promotional campaign was lacklustre. He needn't have worried. The show was a huge overnight phenomenon.

(992) Priah Ferguson's scenes as Erica Sinclair in Stranger Things 2 were slightly expanded because the Duffer Brothers thought she was funny. She would get a considerably larger part in Stranger Things 3.

(993) Hopper and Joyce seem to be at (the dark mirror version of) the Hawkins Library when they rescue will in the Upside Down in the season one finale.

(994) Costume designer Amy Parris said of the food court uniforms in the Starcourt Mall - "People still sell them. We were able to buy two full sets and a third shirt and we made pants to match so we had three original Burger King uniforms. We reached out to Hot Dog on a Stick because they were at the mall and they were in the food court. They were so excited to give us uniforms; in fact, they remade the shirts. They supplied us with the actual uniforms which was really helpful and nice."

(995) The sound design of the Demogorgon took its inspiration from the sound effects that marked the arrival of the Predator in the classic 1987 film.

(996) When she was told the premise of Stranger Things, Millie Bobby Brown asked why Joyce didn't contact Will Byers on his telephone. She was unaware that people didn't carry mobile telephones around with them in 1983.

(997) Will Byers tells Mike in Stranger Things 2 that his

connection to the Upside Down is like a View-Master. View-Master was a popular toy in the eighties. It was essentially like 3-D googles into which you put photographic slides to view. The slides you purchased for the View-Master were usually television and film tie-ins like the Muppets or the latest Hollywood blockbusters.

(998) The scene where Robin and Steve are captivated by the glowing neon lights of the mall roof is a slice of psychedelia with thematic connections to season one (which revolved around the LSD driven MKUltra). This scene is inspired by the tradition of psychedelia in cinema.

(999) The boys refer to "proton packs" on their Ghostbusters costume in Stranger Things 2. This is a mistake because this term was only used in 1989's Ghostbusters II. In 1984 they would have said "positron colliders" rather than proton packs.

(1000) The part of Robin Buckley proved quite tricky to cast and so Joe Keery was brought in to do some auditions with the actresses testing to play Robin in order to make the process more thorough.

(1001) The Duffer Brothers joked that the last ever shot in Stranger Things should be Barb's hand reaching up through her grave.

CPSIA information can be obtained
at www.ICGtesting.com
Printed in the USA
BVHW031645181022
649734BV00013B/447